Nationalism
and Socialism
in the Armenian
Revolutionary
Movement
(1887-1912)

The Zoryan Institute wishes to recognize the moral support and financial contribution of a group of four friends from afar who shared their modest resources with the Institute to make this publication possible and who prefer to remain anonymous.

NATIONALISM AND SOCIALISM IN THE ARMENIAN REVOLUTIONARY MOVEMENT (1887-1912)

Anaide Ter Minassian

Translated by A.M. BERRETT

The Zoryan Institute. Cambridge, Massachusetts 1984

Zoryan Institute
Thematic Series
No. 1

Published by
the kind permission of the author
and Éditions Parenthèses,
Roquevaire, France.

Series Editor
Gerard J. Libaridian

Editorial Assistant
Mark A. Ayanian

Copyright © 1983 Éditions Parenthèses
English Translation Copyright © 1984 by The Zoryan Institute
for Contemporary Armenian Research
and Documentation, Inc.
Cambridge, Massachusetts

Library of Congress Cataloging in Publication Data

*Nationalism and Socialism in the Armenian
Revolutionary Movement (1887-1912)*

LC Number 84-50271
ISBN 0-916431-04-5

*Printed in the United States of America
by The Transcript Printing Company, Peterborough, New Hampshire
Designed by Tatul Sonentz-Papazian*

CONTENTS

Prologue	vi
1. The Facts of the Problem	1
2. A National Populism (1887-1903)	9
3. Time for Choice (1903-1907)	23
4. "The Stolypin Reaction"	51
Notes	57

Prologue

By the nineteenth century, Armenian nationalism had a history that spanned several centuries, if we accept that national consciousness identified with religious and cultural consciousness survived the disappearance of the Armenian principalities and kingdoms.[1] Armenian nationalism involved a minority dwelling on the edges of multinational empires and dispersed in far flung colonies. The manner in which this nationalism was expressed varied from one social class to another (clergy, nobles, merchants, intellectuals, peasants) and according to their cultural characteristics, but at first it was no more than nostalgia for the country of their origins and the certainty that it existed.[2] Under the influence of the revolutions in France and other European countries as well as of the Balkan revolts, Armenian political thought — the thought of intellectuals brought up in contact with the West — was modernized. The idea of the Nation and the People, with all their centripetal implications, slowly emerged from the limits of the religious community, perpetuated well into the nineteenth century by the system of **millets** in the Ottoman Empire and **polozhenye** ("statutes") in the Russian Empire.[3]

Nationalism found its own momentum among the Armenians in Turkey or those in Madras, and it was not a doctrine peculiar to the Armenians in the Caucasus. However, Caucasian Armenians gave it original traits.[4] Seeing the annexation of Transcaucasia by the Russian Empire as a 'liberation,' they weighed the negative aspects of this annexation — autocracy and colonialism — against the positive aspects, i.e., physical security, and the economic and cultural development of Armenians.[5] Until the beginning of the twentieth century, Caucasian Armenian nationalism, in so far as it was the wellspring of political action, was thus condemned to seek its goal outside the Russian Empire.

From 1887 to 1921, when the Treaty of Moscow put an end to the projects for an Armenian national home in Asia Minor, socialism was inseparable from nationalism in the movement for Armenian emancipation.[6] Caucasian Armenians introduced socialism — in the broad sense of the term — into the evolution of the national movement. They also introduced Marxism into it. But Marxism, which spread rapidly among the Georgians, made only slow progress among the Armenians, and only imposed itself as the official ideology after the incorporation of Armenia into the Soviet Union.

Caucasian Armenians set up Pan-Armenian organizations to settle the Armenian Question. Acting as the dynamic element in Armenian society as a whole, they became involved in the revolutionary cycle that developed from Transcaucasia (1905 Revolution) to Persia (constitutional movement from 1906 to 1912) and the Ottoman Empire (Young Turk Revolution of 1908). Westernized and nurtured on the lessons of the French Revolution of 1789 and the European national movements, they concluded that revolution was necessary as the only midwife of modern societies and that its victory was inevitable provided it was based on a popular and national uprising. These certainties dictated the behavior of the radicalized intellectuals: "Make the revolution" wherever possible. They illustrated the problem, which is historically so important, of the contacts between modern and traditional societies. They thus became pioneers of democratic, liberal, and socialist ideas in the East.

From 1887 (foundation of the Hunchak party) to 1912 (when the Russian army restored order in Tabriz) their pragmatism, their hesitations, and their setbacks must be explained in the context of the extensive difficulties they encountered. It must be remembered that, at this time, there was no model of a revolution in the East and all the problems of the East ran through Armenian society: political problems (despotic regimes and Western imperialism), economic problems (underdevelopment, rural economy, corrupt modes of land ownership and agrarian problems), social problems (feudalism among nomadic and sedentary societies, rural exodus), national problems (ethnic diversity), religious problems (predominance of Islam and religious cleavage), and cultural problems (linguistic pluralism, uneven cultural development of Muslim and non-Muslim communities).

1
THE FACTS OF THE PROBLEM

A Dispersed Society

At the end of the nineteenth century the number of Armenians was estimated to be 3,500,000: probably about two-thirds of them lived in the Ottoman Empire.[7] The only certainty concerns the number of Armenians in the Russian Empire; there were 1,240,000 in 1897.[8] Invasions, wars, treaties, and migrations had scattered them among the Ottoman, Russian, and Persian Empires, and a world-wide Diaspora. In addition to language, religion, and script, they had in common a distinctive social structure: a broad peasant base, a relatively developed middle class, a national clergy, and no nobility.[9] The Armenian peasantry, mainly located in historic Armenia as well as in Cilicia and the region of Isfahan, formed a mosaic of communities amidst a host of some Christian but mostly Muslim peoples — Kurds, Turks, Lazes, Circassians, Azeris or Tatars, Persians, Arabs, Georgians, Assyro-Chaldeans, etc.[10] Thus, and it was vital for the future, Armenians nowhere had a true "national" territory.

As in the West, the notion of middle class covered disparate social elements. In the villages, small towns, and cities, the traditional picture of the Armenian artisan or trader was confirmed by the pursuit of ancient crafts and business. From Tabriz to Tiflis, from Van to Constantinople, above the wretched mass of porters, servants, peddlers, and petty clerks, there was the least well-off, but still Asiatic, caste of artisans and bazaar merchants, the impecunious stratum of national intellectuals (journalists, writers, teachers), and the well-to-do and Europeanized members of the liberal professions.

For centuries, a small but very wealthy Armenian bourgeoisie had grown up at the crossroads of international trade at Van and Erzerum,[11] but generally outside Armenia, at Isfahan, Tabriz, Tiflis, Trebizond, Constantinople, Smyrna, and Alexandria.[12] Merchants, money changers, and jewellers spread as far as Madras, Nijni-Novgorod, Marseilles, Antwerp, Amsterdam, London, and Manchester. In Transcaucasia, during the last decades of the nineteenth century, an industrial bourgeoisie appeared. Formed in Tiflis in the cotton, leather, and tobacco sectors, it triumphed in Baku where the Armenian oil pioneers — the Mirzoevs, Ljanozovs, Gukasovs, and Mantashevs — were in the same league as the Nobels and the Rothschilds.[13]

It was also in the industrial centers of Transcaucasia, Baku, Tiflis, and Batum, far from rural Armenia, that the beginnings of an Armenian working class came into being. Driven out by hunger from their villages in Gharabagh, Zangezur, Aderbadakan, Sasun, or Vaspurakan, Armenian artisans and peasants were at first "temporary migrants" who slowly blended into a multinational working class.[14]

The Gregorian or Apostolic Armenian Church was a national institution, in appearance powerful and respected. Closely subordinated to the political authority they fell under, the Catholicos of Etchmiadzin and the Patriarch of Constantinople had secured for themselves recognition of major privileges which made the higher clergy something like a ruling class. But the Armenian Church was going through a profound crisis and the clergy, few in number, saw its political and cultural monopoly disputed by the appearance of a lay intelligentsia.[15]

The dispersion of Armenian society and the gap between

the rural world and the bourgeoisie of the Diaspora amplified the divisions created by political borders and determined the original features of the Armenian revolutionary movement: the populist crusade of the Caucasians toward Ottoman Armenia and their desire to re-establish, between segments of the nation and between social classes, the links broken by history.

The Armenian Question[16]

The Armenian Question was an aspect of the Eastern Question, whose main features it reproduced: an oppressed Christian minority in the Ottoman Empire, the ensuing cultural renaissance, the example of the Balkan revolts, the inability of the Ottoman Empire to modernize itself, and the rivalry of the European powers.

The *Hatt-i-Humayun* of 1856 had proclaimed the legal equality of all Muslim and non-Muslim (*rayah*) subjects of the Ottoman Empire but it had no practical application in the Anatolian provinces. And while the "National Constitution" and the "National Assembly" were real reforms, the main beneficiaries were the Armenian bourgeoisie and clergy in Constantinople; the lot of the Armenian peasantry, like that of the Anatolian peasantry as a whole, continued to worsen.[17]

The agrarian problem was the key feature of the Armenian Question. A centralized Ottoman bureaucracy and a new system of taxes increased the fiscal pressure without abolishing archaic modes of collection, "feudal rent," abuses, corruption, and anarchy in the provinces. Permanently indebted and delivered over to arbitrariness, the Armenian peasants saw their harvests and lands seized by the tax farmers, the usurers (who were often Armenian *aghas*), and the great Muslim landowners.[18] Continuing in accordance with the vagaries of famines and forced economic migrations (*pandukhtutiun*), the dispossession of the peasantry speeded up in the second half of the nineteenth century with the appearance of the Circassians and the expansion of the Kurds.[19]

In fact, the hard-won Russian victory over the Gorcys resulted, after 1864, in the departure of some half a million Caucasian Muslims (Circassians, Abkhazes, Ubykhs, etc.) for the Ottoman Empire.[20] They settled in the provinces along the frontier and as far as Cilicia and were followed by the European *muhajirs*. Both groups often settled on the lands of Armenian *rayahs*.

With the approval of the Turkish authorities, the area allotted to the movement of the nomadic southern Kurds was extended further and further north and northeastward. The Kurds, nomads or semi-nomads, would winter in the regions of Mush, Van, and around Ararat, occupying the towns and villages of sedentarized peoples, demanding upkeep and tribute from the Armenian peasants, forcing them to purchase their protection (*hafir*), pillaging with impunity, and carrying off women and flocks.[21] The usual reactions of the Armenian peasant and artisan were flight and emigration toward Constantinople, Smyrna, and Transcaucasia.

Since the late eighteenth century, Russian expansion toward the Black and the Caspian Seas had revealed the Russophile feelings of the Armenian populations in the Persian and Ottoman provinces: they were the manifestation of an ecumenical Christian consciousness in the face of Islam. Counting on the benevolent protection of the Orthodox Tsar, the ordinary Armenians welcomed each appearance of the Russian army (in 1829, 1854-56, and 1877-78) with demonstrations of joy, followed by more or less sizeable migrations in the direction of Transcaucasia after its incorporation into the Russian Empire (1801-1829).[22] Attitudes of this sort — and the intention attributed to Russian diplomacy to use Armenians as tools in their imperial strategy in Asia Minor — compromised the Armenian community which the Turks had regarded until then as a "loyal community."[23]

The Bulgarian revolt and the Russo-Turkish War (1877-78) as well as the simultaneous appearance of Russian armies on the Euphrates and at the gates of Constantinople created a crisis situation in the Ottoman Empire. This crisis compelled the Armenian Patriarch of Constantinople, Nerses Varjapetian, and the notables in the National Assembly to take action. Their choice — to present the Great Powers with a program of administrative autonomy, inside the Ottoman framework, for the *vilayets* in Turkish Armenia — was dictated by a sincere attachment to the Ottoman Empire, reinforced by misgivings about a possible protectorate by Russia synonymous with Panslavism and Orthodoxy. Article 61 of the Treaty of Berlin (1878), which repeated, but watered down, the promises of Article 16 of the Treaty of San Stefano, internationalized and legitimized the Armenian Question. The task, entrusted to the Porte and to be put into effect under the supervision of the powers, was never carried out. But, for several decades, it kept dangerous illusions alive among Armenian revolutionaries and reformers, and led the Ottoman authorities to believe that Armenians sought the break-up of the Ottoman Empire.

The Awakening of the Armenians in Turkey

The revolt of the Armenians in Zeytun in 1862 and the disturbances in Van and Erzerum in 1863, though limited and spontaneous, were followed by the formation of ephemeral secret societies. Armenians based these societies — the "Union of Salvation" (1872) and the "Black Cross Society" (1878) in Van, the "Protectors of the Fatherland" in Erzerum (1881) — on models provided by the Caucasian Armenians.[24] After 1878, calls for revolt were largely due to the disappointment that followed the "Great Expectations" aroused by Article 61.

It was in Van, in 1885, that the first Armenian revolutionary party was formed.[25] Created by Armenians in Turkey, the Armenakan party drew its membership almost entirely from among them. The Armenakans were democratic and liberal patriots who had a clear perception of the economic and cultural underdevelopment of Asia Minor. But while they sought progress and "national freedom," they called for the use of violence and the arming of the Armenian peasantry for its own self-defense.

The Caucasian Intelligentsia

It was the Caucasian intelligentsia, however, who gave the Armenians their two common revolutionary organizations, the Hunchak party (eventually the *Sotsial-demokratakan Hunchakian Kusaktsutiun*) founded in 1887 in Geneva and the Dashnak party (*Hay Heghapokhakan Dashnaktsutiun*) founded in 1890 in Tiflis. Like its homologue, the Russian intelligentsia, this social group was numerically very weak and it was defined in relation to culture (Armenian, Russian, or Western) and revolutionary ideology.

The first generation of intellectuals, formed in the 1840s and 1850s (later than in Turkey), was that of the sons of good families or scholarship students sent to Russian or European universities. Under the driving spirit of the Armenian clergy who used all the resources of *polozhenye* (1836) and thanks to the gifts of a few rich benefactors, a network of Armenian primary and secondary schools developed in Transcaucasia and the Russian Empire during the second half of the nineteenth century.[26] Recruitment into the schools widened and the second generation of the intelligentsia took shape. Sons of *kahanas*, artisans, and peasants, they were very often only half-educated and self-taught products of the parish and diocesan Armenian schools.

The cleverest ones attended one of the three establishments at the summit of Armenian education in the Russian Empire: the Nersesian Academy in Tiflis,[27] the Gevorgian Academy in Etchmiadzin,[28] and the Lazarev Academy in Moscow.[29] The first and the second were seminaries but acted as teacher-training schools. The latter two recruited their students from as far afield as the Persian and Turkish empires. These nurseries trained the often half-starved contingent of Armenian-language "national" teachers, journalists, and writers, which at the turn of the century was to merge with the contingent of already professional revolutionaries — Hunchaks, Dashnaks, Armenian Social Revolutionaries, and Social Democrats.[30] Above them, at the beginning of the twentieth century, were agronomists, engineers, lawyers, doctors, and a few senior civil servants trained in the technical schools or the universities. Despite their place in Russian society and economic life, some of these professionals retained psychological traits of the intelligentsia.

The intelligentsia, the bearer of Enlightenment (however limited it may have been), had a messianic revolutionary and national vocation: to drag the Armenian people out of its "Asiatic darkness" and economic backwardness, give it back its dignity lost during the centuries of subjection, and inculcate it with a national consciousness and a political will.[31] Revolting against all aspects of oriental despotism, it aspired to the creation of a democratic and civilized society. Despite its horror of all oppression, it acknowledged the civilizing features of tsarist autocracy (rule of law, development of capitalism and culture), proof of which it found in the "social development" of the Armenians in Russia and even in its own existence.

From Kars to Shushi, from Elisabetpol to Baku, the Armenian intelligentsia was placed at the outposts of an Islamic East in which it saw only the present material and cultural inferiority. The European orientation of that intelligentsia was demonstrated by the association of socialism with the Armenian Question. This ideological anticipation of economic and social changes is typical of the acculturated intelligentsia of underdeveloped countries; it is to be explained also by the fact that socialism is perceived as a movement that goes hand in hand with political democracy which would fulfill the promise sprung from the French Revolution — the event above all events for the Armenian intelligentsia — of equality among individuals and equality among nations.

After the forced closure of Armenian schools, in 1885 and 1897,[33] the Eastern Armenian intelligentsia was taught in Russian gymnasia and teacher-training schools, and then enrolled, for lack of a Transcaucasian university, at universities in Moscow, St Petersburg, Dorpat, Leipzig, Berlin, and Geneva.[34] In so doing, it passed through the same populist and Marxist stages as the Russian intelligentsia.

2
A NATIONAL POPULISM (1887-1903)

In 1887, six young Russian Armenian students who knew Plekhanov and thought of themselves as Marxists, founded the Hunchakian Social Democratic Party in Geneva.[35] But it is the influence of the *Narodnaya Volya* ("people's will") which is clearly dominant in their program, organization, and tactics rather than that of Marx. The title of their organ, *Hunchak* (Bell), is the Armenian translation of *Kolokol*. During the summer of 1890, in an environment where small circles of *narodnik*, nationalist, *mshakakan* (followers of the liberal daily *Mshak*), and Hunchakian "Marxist" students and intellectuals came together, the Dashnaktsutiun came into existence.[36]

The Hunchakian and Dashnaktsutiun parties were sociologically identical, had identical objectives (the defense and emancipation of Turkish Armenians), and saw the "Armenian revolution" as a means to activate European diplomacy and advance the political solution of the Armenian Question. But after a brief attempt at union (1890-91), they split on the question of socialism and thenceforth carried on a parallel action.[37]

Socialism and the Hunchaks

The Caucasian Hunchaks were the first to introduce

socialism into the Armenian Question. While their minimum program called for "a broad democracy, political freedom, and national independence" for Turkish Armenia through "insurrectionary revolutionary action," their maximum program denounced the exploitation of man by man and set socialism as the "future objective . . . for the Armenian people and its fatherland."[38]

The Caucasian Hunchaks were also the first — except perhaps for the Anarchists[39] — to concern themselves with problems of propaganda: they undertook the translation into Armenian of a number of socialist writings that were published in their journals *Hunchak* (Bell), *Gaghapar* (Ideas), *Aptak* (Slap), etc.[40] or in the form of pamphlets. The publication of the Armenian translation of Marx's Communist Party Manifesto, begun in 1894, remained unfinished.[41] But, in its early days, Hunchak political thought, literally bogged down in sentiment, was reduced to a turgid and incantatory revolutionary verbiage in which words like "revolution," "revolutionary," "freedom," "despotism," "barbarism," "misery," "humiliation," "sacrifices," and "socialism" recurred with regularity.

The Hunchak party went on the offensive from 1890 through 1896, led autocratically by Avetis and Maro Nazarbekians and a few faithful Caucasians constituted as the "Hunchak Center." This Center moved from Geneva to Paris, then to Athens, and finally to London. The party had a large following from Trebizond to Constantinople among the Armenian intelligentsia in Turkey, stirred up for the "Sacred Task" (*Surb Gords*). The boldness of its actions in the Ottoman Empire[42] — demonstrations in Constantinople, revolts in Sasun and Zeytun — seem to have worried the Young Turks as much as the government.[43] The latter's brutal response — the Armenian massacres of 1894-1896 — did not lead to any intervention by the Great Powers.

At the London Congress of the Hunchak Party (1896), the tactics of the Center came under violent criticism. The Caucasians were placed in a minority by the Hunchaks from Turkey and Egypt who criticized them for linking the Armenian Question to the Russian workers' question, and for thus frightening not only the conservative Armenian bourgeoisie and Muslim society but also the Western capitalist bourgeoisie, which was not at all anxious to support an Armenian socialist movement in the Ottoman Empire. There was a split. The *Verakazmial* (Reconstituted) party was formally founded in London in 1898; it retained only the reformist democratic and national program and drew its membership from Armenians in Turkey, Egypt, and the United States. The Hunchak Center, isolated, gravely weakened, and reduced to its Caucasian elements, retained its socialist and even Marxist label but withdrew from public demonstrations. It survived in Transcaucasia and in Bulgaria.

The Dashnak Manifesto

The very name of the Dashnaktsutiun ("Federation") party is a reminder that it was born, in 1890, of the federation in Tiflis of small Caucasian revolutionary groups which had become convinced of the need to unite weak and divided forces. It thus sought to welcome into its ranks all Armenians, nationalists or socialists, moderates or radicals, who sought the "political and economic freedom of Turkish Armenia." The majority envisaged a democratic and liberal revolution, but the minority, which included the *narodniks*, was socialist.[44]

Until 1892, the Dashnak party slowly organized itself and functioned without a program. From its early days there remains only a naive and patriotic *Manifesto* calling on all Armenians — including the young, the old, the rich, the women, the priests — to support the "people's war" and the "Sacred Task" against the Turkish government.[45] The absence in the *Manifesto* of socialism as a goal was explained in the first issue of *Droshak* (Flag), the official organ of the Dashnak party, in terms of the impossibility of adopting as an objective "a social organization for which a struggle can at present be waged only in Western Europe."[46] There were no industries and no factories in Turkey; agriculture and traditional ways of life predominated; and the cultural level was low, argued the *Droshak*. While "there can be no question of (European) socialism," *Droshak* intended to struggle for the people's "welfare" and against everything that stifled national growth.

However, from 1892 to 1907, socialism was to remain as it were the bad conscience of the Dashnak party. The First Congress, held secretly in Tiflis in 1892, finally gave the party a formal program. For the first time, delegates from Turkish Armenia were present, knowing nothing about socialism. Their presence, combined with the desire for immediate action, are enough to explain why theoretical issues were neglected in favor of problems of organization and tactics. Despite that, the Caucasian left wing, led by the triumvirate of Kristapor Mikayelian, Stepan Zorian, and Simon Zavarian, succeeded in getting socialism accepted in a visionary Preamble "without mentioning the word," as a general principle and ultimate ideal, conditional upon the victory of the proletariat in the advanced countries.[47]

Despite the looseness of the sociological concepts and the orientalisms of political language, there was an attempt to apply the categories of the social question to the national problem through the identification of oppositions between "conquerors/subjects," "Turks/Christians," "exploiters/exploited," and the concrete proposal to end all existing forms of oppression in the Ottoman Empire. The eleven-point political program was extremely moderate: the establishment of democratic freedoms in Turkish Armenia through revolutionary action. There was no question of political autonomy or independence, still less of the unification of the three Armenias (as proposed by the Hunchaks). What the program proposed was the development of popular culture and economic activities. Tactics (psychological action, combat groups, terrorism) and organization (revolutionary committees), envisaged in a decentralized way, figured prominently in the document.[48]

The Dashnaks too hoped that the Powers would intervene on behalf of the Armenian movement. They had not failed to notice that the freedom of the Balkan peoples from Ottoman dominion was not the result of the activities of Greek, Rumanian, Serbian, or Bulgarian *haiduks*, whose heroism counted for little against the Turkish army, but of the intervention of one or several European Powers.[49] Even after the repression of 1894-1896, observing that demoralization, fear, and reaction were the dominant feelings among the Armenians, Mikayelian played down the risks of such tactics, on the grounds that through Article 61 the Armenian people had "become . . . the ally of the six contracting Powers."[50] And, indeed, most of the efforts of the Caucasians who staffed the Western Bureau or headquarters of the Dashnaktsutiun in Geneva were directed toward reminding the European states of their promises, their duties, and the justice of the Armenian cause — an approach that the Social Democrat Bashkhi Ishkhanian was later to describe as "political beggary."[51]

Toward a Progressive Politics

But in the late 1890s, the Dashnaks, like the Hunchaks, without yet having a very clear conception of the contradictions running through the Armenian Question (Franco-Russian alliance, Anglo-Russian rivalry, Germano-Turkish rapprochement, etc.), noted the impact of European economic and financial imperialism in the Ottoman Empire. They sought to distance themselves from capitalist Europe by winning the backing of European workers and socialists repelled by the massacres. Both parties, therefore, placed increasing value on the socialist aspect of their programs.

Moreover, to be recognized by and represented in the Second International was the aim of all the small socialist parties. The Caucasian Hunchaks were concerned about such an affiliation as early as in 1889. Plekhanov, whom they knew personally, had been representing them formally in the International since the Paris Congress. He remained their correspondent even after 1905, despite the accusations of nationalism made against them.[52]

From 1896 onward, the Dashnaks, who for two years had been embarked on the translation and publication of socialist pamphlets, turned up at all the Congresses of the Second International. Karl Liebknecht, who was faithful to the lessons of Marx and Engels to struggle against tsarism rather than against the territorial integrity of the Ottoman Empire, suspected that Armenian revolutionaries were, in objective terms, the agents of Russian expansionism in Asia Minor. But the revolutionaries had the support of Rosa Luxemburg. She turned the Marxist thesis on its head and showed that the development of economic and social forces, the essential prerequisite for the development of social democracy in the Ottoman Empire, went through the national movement and the emancipation of the Christian peoples.[53] The Dashnaks had strong and convinced supporters of the Armenian cause in Jean Jaurès, J. Longuet, Emil Vandervelde, Henri Van Kol, Camille Huysmans, Karl Kautsky, August Bebel, Edward Bernstein, and other prominent socialists. The launching of *Pro Armenia* in 1900 was the outcome of collaboration between the Dashnaks (who financed and published it) and French democratic and socialist leaders (George Clemenceau, Anatole France, Jean Jaurès, F. de Pressensé, E. de Roberty, J. Longuet, Pierre Quillard).[54]

In 1901, at the request of the Dashnaks, the International Socialist Bureau (ISB) called on socialists to act in their respective parliaments and intervene with their respective governments to put an end to the massacres.[55] This appeal shows, beyond humanitarian considerations, the gradually increasing sensitivity of the Second International to the national question.

A Theoretical Gap

The revolutionary impatience ("act and act now") of the Hunchaks and the Dashnaks and organizational problems during the decade 1887-1897 prevented serious theoretical reflection, reduced to the publication of popular and propaganda articles in the party press. Nationalism drew its arguments from Armenian literature (Mikayel Nalbandian, Ghevond Alishan, Mkrtich Beshiktashlian, Kamar Katiba, Raffi), socialism from the translation of a number of German, French, and Russian "classics" of European socialism.

Complete ideological unification among individuals and small revolutionary groups was neither achieved nor necessary. In the difficult conditions of the struggle, it was enough to agree on immediate objectives.[56] What mattered then, were the models that inspired the action of Armenian militants; Russian populism and the Bulgarian way.

Russian populism shaped the outlook of the Armenian intelligentsia and determined the forms of its action.[57] From the Russo-Turkish War (1877-78) and the foundation of the Narodnaya Volya to the assassination of Alexander II (1881), populism attracted a small minority of Armenian school and university students in Tiflis, Moscow, and St Petersburg.

Some of the founders of the Hunchak and Dashnak parties had moved in populist circles (Maro Vardanian, Gevork Kharajian) and even belonged to the Narodnaya Volya (Kristapor Mikayelian, Abraham Dastakian, Simon Zavarian). In Tiflis, the Committee of the Narodnaya Volya in 1880 had six members (three Armenians and three Georgians) who spoke in Russian and struggled for popular freedom in the Russian Empire. However, the majority of the young Armenian activists (mostly students at the Nersesian Academy) belonged to small illegal groups, formed on the model of the famous *krujki*, which met to read the works of the radical Russian intelligentsia, from Belinski to Pisarev, and above all those of Armenian writers.[58] In the eighties these groups analyzed the writings of Mikayel Nalbandian, a friend of Herzen, and articles in the legal Armenian liberal organ *Mshak*, whose editor, Grigor Ardsruni, was a convinced "Westernizer." One could get carried away by Kamar Katipa's poems and Raffi's novels.[59]

The role of national literature in the psychological and ideological formation of those who were to become militants or professional revolutionaries must be stressed. Many of them would be poets or writers at the same time. In terms of influence exercised, none can compare with Raffi (1835-1888), a prolific and romantic writer whose work was inspired by episodes drawn from Armenian history. Raffi set off in his young readers an impassioned energy, a thirst for freedom and sacrifice, and an exaltation of the Ego — all mixed with an almost neurotic love for Western Armenia, the captive and sullied Motherland that must be freed. In 1880 Raffi released his novel *Khente* (The Fool) in which he created prophetically the model of the "new Armenian man," the revolutionary.

Along the Path of Populism

Whatever the strength of imitation, Caucasian Armenian young men could not accept fully the objectives of Russian populism: to construct socialism on the basis of the rural commune and to overthrow the autocracy. Certainly, serious agrarian problems did exist in Transcaucasia, especially in Georgia, but also in regions where the Armenian peasantry was disputing possession of land and water with Muslim landowners, the *aghalar* and *mulkadar*. There existed communal lands and forms of appropriation of land that were favorable to the producers ("Land belongs to the tiller"), but there was no *mir* (communal village). As for the autocracy, it might be feared and even hated, but, when compared to Oriental despotisms, it still appeared as a civilizing order and the sole bulwark against the Turkish menace. Finally, Russian populism, a profoundly national and Slavophile movement, provided no solution to the national problems of non-Russian elements.

But the Armenian intelligentsia, radicalized by contact with Russian political thought and convinced by Lavrov of the duty of total sacrifice to the people, transposed the behavior of the Russian intelligentsia to a national key. The famous "V Narod" (Go to the People) became the "*depi Erkir*"[61] (Toward the Homeland) of Armenian patriots. The *Erkir* (Homeland) described historic Armenia inside the borders of the Ottoman Empire. It was the legendary fatherland with its people (*zhoghovurd*) of oppressed and fatalistic peasants and artisans who formed the core of the nation (*azg*).

The Russo-Turkish War of 1877-78, in which Caucasian Armenians participated actively, the Russian annexation of Kars, Artahan, and Batum, and the departure with the Russian army of thousands of Armenian peasants from Turkey were the occasion for contacts and discoveries. The Caucasian press and literature wrote of the harsh reality in the *Erkir*: the wretchedness and sufferings of its people as well as the violence of social relations. They kept alive the bad conscience of a number of sensitive young men who, like the Russian "repentant nobility," became aware of their duties as they became aware of their privileges: to bring justice and freedom to the people of the *Erkir*.

The failure of the populists after the assassination of Alexander II, adding to the disappointments following the Congress of Berlin, helped to cut off the Caucasian Armenian intelligentsia from the Pan-Russian movement and to turn it toward national goals. At the beginning of 1882, while the Georgian movement was developing as an internationalist movement (struggling with the peoples of the Empire against the autocracy) and rapidly absorbing Marxism,[61] Armenians on the Narodnaya Volya committee split away in Tiflis and formed an organization that "devoted all its activity to the interests of the unhappy Armenian people," which was echoed in Moscow by the establishment of a secret center.[62] Its name, "Union of Patriots" (*Hayrenaserneri miutiun*), summarized its program.[63]

The closure of Armenian schools in the Caucasus from 1885 to 1886 was the occasion for the first tract ever drawn up in Armenian against tsarism.[64] The closure exacerbated national feelings and above all made Armenian teachers available for other purposes.

The "crusade" toward the *Erkir* was imposed on Pan-Armenian organizations by the fact that the country was divided. It commanded Caucasian revolutionaries to act outside Russia in the Ottoman Empire. It turned aside, isolated, and cut off Armenians in the Caucasus from their Georgian and Russian neighbors at the very moment when Marxism was making its appearance among them.

The Armenian crusade repeated, in a telescoped form, the stages of Russian populism. The peaceful crusade of traveling "pilgrims" who turned themselves into geographers, ethnographers, or linguists for the occasion, revealing Turkish Armenia to their readers in Tiflis, was followed by Kukunian's armed crusade prefiguring the *fedayee* movement.

The Bulgarian Way

During the summer of 1890, at the time when the Dashnak party was being founded in Tiflis, an armed expedition of

125 very young men led by a student from St Petersburg, Sargis Kukunian, attempted to cross the Ottoman frontier.[65] It was a disastrous failure. But their "heroism" and their watchword ("We are going to die to free our brothers"), popularized in songs and iconography, had a profound impact among Armenians who were thus offered a second model, the Bulgarian one.

Undoubtedly, the Bulgarian revolution, occurring at the same time as the Armenian Question, inspired the Caucasian revolutionaries' tactics. Armenian political writings discussed and analyzed its course ad infinitum: the *haiduk* movement, the popular uprising, "Bulgarian atrocities," parliamentary questions in the West, Russian intervention, and autonomy for Bulgaria. The Bulgarian model, which reflected the specific experiences of the Balkans, was thus transplanted into Asia Minor. Armenians were a minority on their own territory, however; this ruled out the crucial stage of the popular uprising.[66] Moreover, the Armenian Question erupted at a time (the early nineties) when changes in international diplomacy had turned Asia Minor into a strategically less important area.

Intervention by Russia, which was turning to the Far East, had become unlikely. Far from supporting the Armenian revolutionaries, the tsarist government was harassing them severely. The Hunchaks, hostile to the autocracy, were the first to denounce the dangers of a Russian intervention which might have ended in the annexation of Turkish Armenia.[67] Until 1903 the Dashnaks had a more ambiguous attitude. They denounced the policy of Russification and the "white massacre" of Armenians in Russia; but, pointing to the material impossibility of fighting on two fronts, they did not take part in the struggle against tsarism.

The Bulgarian model, inapplicable in reality, condemned the Armenian movement to being no more than a Christian minority movement within the Ottoman Empire. Coming late when compared to the unfolding of events in the Balkans but early in relation to the awakening of the peoples of the East, the Armenian revolution, whatever the dose of socialism injected into it, developed as a national movement, ran up against the incomprehension and hostility of the

Muslim masses, and enclosed the Armenian revolutionaries in a dangerous isolation. Their first attempt to recruit Muslims (especially Kurds and Young Turks) ran foul of religious and ethnic differences, economic and cultural inequalities, and in fact a whole gamut of contempt.[68]

The Rise of the Fedayee

The rapid establishment by the Caucasian Armenians of a network of rival Hunchak and Dashnak committees in Transcaucasia, the Ottoman Empire, Persia, the Balkans, and even the United States resulted in the creation of a dual Pan-Armenian political organization, which exists to the present day. But in Armenian folk memory, **the revolutionary movement is identified with the** *fedayee* **movement.** *Fedayee* is a term borrowed from Persian. It means "he who is committed" or "he who is sacrificed."[69] This movement was a forerunner of the freedom fighters from Iran to Algeria in the twentieth century Muslim world.

The Armenian *fedayee* was born of the people. Whether Caucasian or Ottoman intellectual, priest or simple peasant, he was an armed revolutionary who dedicated his life to the people whom he awakened by the example of his deeds and his death. While it is true that he bore within him some of the traits bequeathed by the Russian populists, the Garibaldists, and the Bulgarian *haiduk*, he was also the heir to an earlier Armenian rural banditry.

Organized in mobile bands of 10 to 15 armed men, the *fedayee* avoided any offensive action which might provoke reprisals. At the same time, he helped peasants **defend themselves in Turkey.** That implied the occurrence of what can only be described as a psychological revolution among the *rayah*, who had been crushed down by centuries-old fear, passivity, and fatalism. The peasant had to be taught to resist and to dare to defend himself against the Kurd, the Turkish official, and the Armenian usurer. To give him the means to dare, the peasant had to be armed. But "arming the people" was more a slogan than a reality, since insoluble problems of financing and logistics (*fedayee*, arms, and munitions crossed through Transcaucasia and Persia) never made it possible to go beyond the limits of guerrilla action restricted to a few mountainous areas. The general uprising that Hunchaks had thought possible, but that Dashnaks had not put into their program, turned out to be impossible: the Sasun uprising, organized by the Hunchaks Tamatian and Poyajian, ended in the massacres of 1894-96.[70] At the same time, the Dashnak party was showing a growing obsession with the problems which are today known as those of revolutionary warfare in Third World countries: revolutionary teaching, armed struggle, worship of violence, and ideological simplification.

The Bourgeoisie: A Missing Link

Finally, the Armenian experience disproves the Marxist theories that every national movement originates with a bourgeoisie in quest of a national market. The Armenian bourgeoisie, supported by the higher clergy, supported "national benevolence" (foundation of cultural and religious institutions and hospitals) and was hostile to the Armenian revolutionaries. As a Diaspora class, the Armenian bourgeoisie in Constantinople, Smyrna, Trebizond, Tiflis, Baku, Tabriz, Isfahan, or Cairo had access to the vast Ottoman, Russian, and Persian imperial markets and was not interested much in the Armenian highlands situated away from the main modern trade routes. Whether conservative or liberal, the Armenian bourgeoisie was always careful to stay in the good books of the government authorities and was not a rebellious class. In the Ottoman Empire, it wished only for reforms. In the Russian Empire, it sought to retain and expand the advantages won as a result of the developments of capitalism and the oil boom. In their press, both Hunchaks and Dashnaks endlessly denounced the self-centeredness of these "Croesuses" who were indifferent to the fate of the nation. The fact that revolutionaries were driven to use terrorism to extract from the bourgeoisie the funds necessary to continue the struggle is sufficient proof that the revolutionary movement expressed the interests of the ruined and oppressed popular classes rather than of the bourgeoisie.[71]

The social origin of the militants (intelligentsia, artisans, peasants), the integration of socialism into nationalism, and the confusion of people and nation make it possible to characterize the Armenian movement as **national populism.**

3
TIME FOR CHOICE
(1903-1907)

Class Struggle or National Struggle?

Until the beginning of the twentieth century, the Armenian revolution was entirely directed against the Ottoman Empire and Armenians in the Caucasus showed no signs of rebellion against the Russian autocracy. Suddenly, the movement's center of gravity was transferred to Transcaucasia, raising the terrible problem of setting new goals. Study of the facts makes it possible to bring out four causes: the deadlock of the Armenian Question, the development of capitalism in Transcaucasia and its resulting social changes, the confiscation of Armenian Church property, and the 1905 Revolution.

Armenian Question Deadlocked

By 1900, the emancipation of Armenians in the Ottoman Empire had not progressed at all. Apathy and demoralization had overtaken Armenians in the Caucasus, in contrast to their enthusiasm of the early nineties. The massacres of 1984-96 claimed 300,000 Armenian victims and led only to feeble diplomatic protests from the Powers. Far from supporting the agitation of Armenian revolutionaries in Asia Minor, Russia suspected them of being manipulated by the British. The tsarists feared that the taste for autonomy might take root among the Armenians and Georgians on the Russian side of the frontier.[72] Faced with the problems of responsibility and failure, the Armenian revolutionary parties marked time. The reformed wing of the Hunchak party still had branches and a press (especially in the communities of the Diaspora) but no practical revolutionary activity in the Ottoman Empire. The Hunchak "Center" continued to exist and even set itself up in the suburban and industrial area of Baku, where Armenian workers at Bibi-Eibat, Surakhani, and Balakhani were concentrated. Since its last exploit in 1897 — the raid by Armenian *fedayees* on Khanasor — the Dashnak party confined itself to Asia Minor, especially in the area of Vaspurakan and Taron, where it performed organizational tasks. The Dashnaks also operated in Western Europe where they carried out their propaganda work. In the Russian Empire, the party established a network of committees in Kars, Alexandrapol, Tiflis, Erevan, Baku, Batum, Nor-Nakhichevan, and Moscow, but faced the growing lack of interest among Caucasians in activities in the Ottoman Empire.

Capitalism in Transcaucasia

Since the late 1860s, capitalism slowly penetrated into Transcaucasia. The construction of railways (especially the Baku-Batum and Rostov-Baku lines) broke the isolation of the region and facilitated its agricultural as well as industrial development. Between 1898 and 1901, under the impact of international, Russian, and Armenian high finance, Baku became the world's leading oil producer. Manganese at Shiaturi, coal at Tkvibuli, copper at Zangezur were exploited as well by numerous small firms. Large-scale exploitation, such as of copper at Allaverdi by a French company, was exceptional. Processing industries developed in the framework of small and medium-sized business, like tobacco at Sukhimi, brandy at Erevan, silk spinning and weaving in Georgia, and, more rarely, of large-scale businesses, like cotton at Tiflis and Baku. Despite the invasion of the Caucasus by Russian manufactured goods (including cotton, sugar, iron, and firearms), long-established handicraft industries (renowned for their firearms, metal articles, clothes, and leathergoods) suffered an uneven decline and even fought back in some sectors, still employing up to 30 percent of the population in Gharabagh.[73]

Industrial development led to the appearance of a working class whose links with the village and household workshop were not broken. This emerging class was concentrated in a number of proletarian oases surrounded by the teeming world of artisans and small businesses: in the railway stations and depots where some 20,000 mostly Russian rail workers were employed in 1908;[74] in Tiflis, promoted to the rank of an administrative, cultural, commercial, and industrial capital, where the workers' world was still tinted with the colors of the oriental bazaar; in Batum, where the barreling factories for the export of petroleum were located; and finally in Baku (only 15,000 inhabitants in 1870 and 214,000 by 1913) which in 1908, with its 178 factories and its 48,699 workers, constituted the only true workers' stronghold in the Caucasus.[75] By virtue of its multinational composition (nearly 20 nationalities), and its stratification, in which "nationality reinforced class," the working class of Baku encapsulated all the characteristics of the Transcaucasian working class.[76] For instance, in the late nineties, the Baku working class was composed from top to bottom of Russian skilled workers (17 to 20 percent of the total), Armenian workers (25 to 29 percent), Azeri or Tatar (12 to 13 percent), and Iranian (19 to 21 percent) laborers.[77]

At the turn of the century Armenians clearly made up the largest national contingent among Baku workers and, until 1917, Baku was the leading Armenian worker center. This fact calls for a number of remarks on the evolution of Armenian society. The outstanding study in the comparative sociology of the Caucasian peoples carried out by the specifist B. Ishkhanian indicates that Armenian society, influenced by the effects of urbanization and industrialization, was distinctly more differentiated in 1897 than Georgian or

Azeri society, and that it was a Diaspora.[78] Although numerically the third largest national group in the Caucasus with 12 percent of the total population, Armenians did not really have a territory. Even in the region of Erevan where 40 percent of the Armenians in the Caucasus were concentrated, they comprised only 53 percent of the population or scarcely more than the Muslims. While 79 percent of Armenians were still rural-dwellers, 21 percent of them — the highest percentage among the peoples of the Caucasus — were city-dwellers. Nearly 200,000 Armenians were concentrated in Tiflis and 52,233 Armenians lived in Baku.[79] A working class was in the making at one end of this city dweller world and a powerful commercial and industrial bourgeoisie at the other.

The embryonic working class formed in emigration and exile. The surplus male labor of the Armenian villages in Gharabagh, Zangezur, Lori, eastern Anatolia, and Iranian Azerbaijan was drained toward Baku, the Promised Land, where a few bold ones would make their fortunes but where the vast majority would swell the ranks of the oil workers (12,000 Armenian workers in 1903); toward Tiflis, where Armenians formed the majority of workers in the tobacco industry and a considerable percentage of workers in the leather and textile industries; and toward Batum, where the wretched escapees from the massacres of 1895 huddled.[80] The only notable concentration of workers in an Armenian province was in Lori: by 1905 4,000 to 5,000 people, a third of whom were Armenians, worked in Allaverdi.[81] Few in number (30,000 for the whole of Transcaucasia in 1910) and scattered, Armenian workers were nomads between their villages and the factories, following the rhythm of the season as well as agricultural or industrial crises.[82] The obstacle of language and religion raised insurmountable barriers to their integration into a unified Transcaucasian working class.

The Armenian bourgeoisie was an old and economically powerful class. It originated in Tiflis, as well as in Astrakhan and Moscow, from the capitalism of the *hoja* or merchant class during the seventeenth and eighteenth centuries.[83] In the nineteenth century, Armenians developed capital by supplying the Russian armies during the Caucasus wars, from trading sugar and cotton goods with Persía, then from the cotton, leather, and tobacco industries they dominated in Tiflis, and ultimately from banking. But it was at Baku, inseparable from the petroleum industries that it had helped to create, that Armenian industrial high finance flourished. Armenians were the pioneers of this area since from 1850 to 1872 the Mirzoev and Gukasov families had a virtual monopoly on Baku petroleum while other Armenian industrialists extended their activities from extraction to the refining, transport, and marketing of petroleum internationally. The wealth of the Lyanozov, Gukasov, Mantashev, and others became legendary.[84]

Capital and Culture

An ancient eastern tradition obliged these *nouveaux riches* to assume the functions of national patrons and philanthropists. The Armenian Church, to which they remained very attached, encouraged them to do more and more good works and to found cultural institutions, but also to hire Armenian workers. Thus, under the cloak of charity, the Armenian capitalist, just like the Muslim capitalist, exploited essentially the workers of his own community. With Armenian managers running the firms, Armenian workers perceived the boss, until the crisis of 1901-1903, as a benefactor, who dispensed jobs and pay. This vague feeling of religious and national solidarity prevented the emergence of a class consciousness. It was the same with the Azeri workers, whereas for the Georgian workers of Baku, Tiflis, and Batum, in the absence of a Georgian industrial bourgeoisie, the owner was always a foreigner and very often an Armenian. Accordingly, class consciousness among Georgians emerged all the more quickly because it went hand in hand with national consciousness and xenophobia.[85]

The economic depression of 1901-1903 deeply affected Transcaucasia, where over-equipped industrial regions coexisted with a traditional rural economy. Between 1900 and 1903 economic strikes paralyzed the railway workers, the peasants, and above all the multinational and semiproletarianized workers in Tiflis, Rostov-on-Don, Baku, Batum, and the province of Guria. Under the influence of the Tiflis, Baku, and Batum committees — established between 1901 and 1902 by Russian, Georgian, and Armenian Social Democrats — the strikes became politicized. There was also a new factor: the spontaneous participation of Armenian workers in Baku and Tiflis in these strikes.

During the nineties, the Hunchak and Dashnak parties, whose existence had preceded the appearance of the labor movement and whose socialism had not benefited from contact with reality, paid only slight attention to the Caucasian labor question. Certainly, the influence of the Hunchaks was as clear as that of the Georgian revolutionaries in the "Mesame-dase" (the Third Group) on the Revolutionary Armenian Workers' Association, founded in Tiflis during 1892.[86] While the Association set as its goal the defense of the economic and political interests of the working class and put forward a program inspired by that of the labor circles of the Narodnaya Volya, it paid particular attention to the national question and the fate of Armenians in Turkey. It hoped to establish a free Armenia, *Azat Hayastan*, which was also the name of its organ. It succeeded in creating a number of groups at Alexandrapol, Kars, Gantzak, and Baku (1894-95) before being broken up by the police in 1895.

Origins of Marxist Tradition

The Marxist Armenian Workers' Group, founded in Tiflis in 1898 and disbanded in 1901, took a significant step forward by linking the fate of the Armenian worker to that of the proletariat of Transcaucasia and Russia.[87] While the "Group" was only a tiny handful of people and its organization was still national, it was no longer isolated. It was in touch with progressive Georgian workers in Tiflis; two of its members — Gevork Gharadjian (Archomedes), a former Hunchak and future Menshevik, and Melik Melikian (Dedushka), a future Bolshevik — belonged to the Social Democratic (SD) group in Tiflis. The new organization took part in strikes in tobacco, leather, and shoe factories where Armenians were a majority. Finally, it abandoned the national question, the question of Turkish Armenia, which it blamed for the isolation of the Armenian worker. In its handwritten organ *Banvor* (*Worker*), the "Group" criticized Hunchaks and Dashnaks alike for their narrow national struggles and proposed strengthening the international character of the Transcaucasian movement.

From 1898 to 1902, it was on this internationalist basis (Russians, Georgians, and Armenians) that tiny Social Democratic groups (sometimes with only 2 or 3 members) began to appear.[88] However, only a handful of Armenian intellectuals, ex-students, and workers adhered to Marxism. The latter (Esalem, Dedushka, Khumarian) came from earlier labor organizations, but the former also had often made a similar journey. Born in the late seventies, they were about 20 years old. Some had attended Armenian parochial schools or the Nersesian Academy and even fleetingly belonged to Hunchak or Dashnak youth groups. The closure of Armenian schools turned these youths to the Russian schools. It was in the higher educational establishments in Moscow, St. Petersburg, Riga, or Dorpat that they were initiated into the Russian revolutionary movement and Marxism. When they were expelled from their institutions during the university disturbances of 1901-1902, they were exiled to Transcaucasia. Few but very active, they demonstrated technical skills when the SD committees in Tiflis and Baku were being formed (1901-1902). They were couriers (carrying the proofs of *Iskra*, the organ of the Russian Social-Democratic Party or RSDWP edited by Lenin, from Tabriz to Ardabil and then to Baku); organizers (such as Bogdan Gnuniantz, and his brothers and sister in Baku); clandestine printers (Dedushka in Baku, Kamo in Tiflis); and factotums (the "legendary" Kamo).[89]

The arrival in Tiflis during the spring of 1902 of a young student expelled from the Riga Polytechnic Institute, Stepan Shahumian, occurred a few months before the creation of the Union of Armenian Social Democrats. The publication of the sole issue of *Proletariat* is the only concrete evidence of the existence of this "Union," whose rather confused *Manifesto* caught Lenin's attention abroad. He asked for everything in *Proletariat* about nationalism and federalism to be translated for him, and congratulated it in *Iskra* "for its correct way of posing the national question."[90]

The "Union," a **separate organization** of Armenian Social Democrats, did not last long. It disappeared when it merged in March 1903 with the Caucasian Union of the RSDWP, a **unitary organization** of Caucasian Social Democrats which included representatives of the Tiflis, Baku, and Batum committees as well as the editorial boards of the Georgian *Brztola* (Struggle) and the Armenian *Proletariat*.[91] The Caucasian Union approved the RSDWP program put forward by *Iskra*, appointed delegates to the second congress of the party, and decided to combine the Georgian and Armenian organs into a single propaganda organ, *Proletariati Krive* (The Proletariat's Struggle). The new organ was published in three editions — Georgian, Armenian, and Russian but, significantly, not in Turkish. The "Outline Program for the Caucasian Union of the RSDWP," published in the first issue, was in conformity with the Iskrist conception of organization and propaganda: a unitary party organization and the use of national languages for the dissemination of Marxist literature. But on the national question, which was a burning one for this mixture of peoples, it revealed Austro-Marxist influence. By proposing the transformation of Russia into a federal democratic republic on the basis of territorial autonomy and the right of secession as the solution, the Caucasian Social Democrats showed that they had read and understood the Brün program (1899). A few months later, at the London congress, Plekhanov and Lenin were united in their rejection of the "Outline" and its unacceptable federalism.[92]

Their limited success with Armenian workers over whom the Dashnaks mounted guard and their obsession with nationalism, which divided and scattered the workers' strength, should be enough to explain the verbal violence of the Armenian Marxists against the Hunchak and Dashnak parties denounced as bourgeois. They severely criticized the poverty of Dashnak ideology which consisted in awakening the spirit of sacrifice of Russian youth which was then dragged into sterile and murderous adventures in Turkey. During a 1901 public debate in Baku between Kristapor Mikayelian, the representative of the Dashnak Western Bureau, and the young Social Democrat Bogdan Gnuniantz, the terms of a debate were set which henceforth were not to change. Gnuniantz criticized the Dashnaks for preventing any political action by Armenians in Russia as well as for ignoring the notion of surplus value and the exploitation of the proletariat. Mikayelian countered with the concept of a "proletarian people." Doubly oppressed — as worker and as nation — the Armenian people was shedding in Turkey the "surplus value of its blood."[93] This facile response could not, however, conceal the fact that there was no longer any unity in the ranks of the Caucasian Dashnaks, especially in Baku, at a time of a rise of political conflicts in Russia.

Church Properties Confiscated

The deadlock in the Armenian Question and the development of the labor movement in Transcaucasia was precipitating among the Hunchak and Dashnak intelligentsia a critical reflection on the nature of the Armenian revolutionary movement (nationalism or socialism?), on its tactics (Bulgarian way or multinational struggle?), and on its strategy (autonomy, independence, or democratization of the Russian and Ottoman empires?). But at that very same time, the Russian governmental decree on the Confiscation of the Property of the Armenian Church provoked a sharp outburst of nationalism.[94]

This decree, proposed by Governor Golitsyn and enacted by Von Plehve, deprived the Church, the only institution common to all Armenians, of its property, which in fact was not very substantial. Yet, this action was the last in a series of measures that were clearly aimed at stifling Armenian culture. During the summer of 1903 peasants, artisans, workers, traders, and intellectuals rebelled spontaneously. The resistance at first took the form of peaceful religious processions and funeral processions which brought together weeping men, women, and children in the Armenian villages. Then the emotion became anger. Demonstrations were stepped up, became hostile to the autocracy (something new), led to confrontations which left some dead and wounded, and finally, on September 2, 1903, took an insurrectional turn in Baku.[95] Though entirely separate in its causes, the Armenian resistance coincided with the general strike of the summer of 1903. In Rostov-on-Don, but above all in Baku, there were numerous Armenian strikes. In contrast to the calm of the Muslims, the tsarist bureaucracy, taken by surprise, tended to treat rebels and Armenians as one and the same. A state of emergency was proclaimed: hundreds of arrests were made at all levels of the Armenian population.

The Hunchaks, Dashnaks, and Social Democrats were also surprised by this sudden awakening of Armenians in the Caucasus. Created by the Dashnak party in the summer of 1903, the Armenian Central Committee for Self-Defense tried to coordinate the hitherto spontaneous popular movements and assumed leadership over them.[96] More than a mere matter of tactics, **self-defense of Armenian communities** became a policy of the Dashnak party and won it unprecedented popularity in Transcaucasia.

Finally, in Tiflis during October 1903, the attempted assassination of Prince Golitsyn by three young Hunchaks was the beginning of a long series of terrorist actions against tsarist officials and the somewhat ill-defined category of "traitors." From 1904, and especially in 1905, Dashnak terrorists replaced Hunchak terrorists but the latter had already won support among workers for the moribund Hunchak party.[97] Between 1903 and 1905, the Hunchak branches in Baku (25 new groups of 15 to 25 members), Erevan, and Alexandrapol saw an influx of members.[98] Thus, by the autumn of 1903, the policy of Russification had driven ordinary Caucasian Armenians into the arms of the revolutionary national parties whose objectives lay in Turkey. For the Marxists, this was a disaster: the Hunchak and Dashnak parties were using nationalism, isolating the Armenian workers by their tactics and their strategy to smother their class consciousness just when the revolutionary movement was getting under way in Russia. The Hunchaks constantly called for class struggle, without resolving the tensions that it created within the national struggle. Faced with the Russian, Georgian, and Armenian Marxists, the Dashnaks rejected class struggle. For them, the extreme dispersal of the Armenian nation, its numerical weakness, and the inequality of the forces facing each other made the alliance of all classes in society essential during the initial phase of national emancipation.

The Russian Revolution, the first signs of which were visible in Transcaucasia in 1903, was to oblige Armenian Marxists, socialists, and nationalists to face squarely the contradictions between class struggle and national struggle. Specifism was the first attempt to resolve this contradiction.

The Challenge of the Specifists

During the turmoil of the spring and summer of 1903, a second group of Caucasian Armenian students became Social Democrats. They differed from the Marxists of *Proletariat* in that they adhered to the perfectly orthodox and somewhat academic Marxism of Plekhanov and Kautsky, which they had discovered in German and Swiss universities, and especially in that they had a greater awareness of the national question. Some were defectors from the Dashnak party (Alexander Rubeni). Others, defectors from the Hunchak party (David Ananun, Sarkis Kasian), had drifted toward Marxism as a result of working on *Veradsnutiun* (Renaissance) published in Ruschuk (Bulgaria) by Avetis Nazarbekian.[99]

In desperation about the impasse in which the Armenian Question found itself and impressed by the strikes of 1903, these students joined the RSDWP committees, only to leave them immediately. The split, finalized at the end of October 1903, resulted in the creation of the Social Democratic Armenian Workers Organization (SDAWO). The reasons adduced were the rejection of some of the resolutions of the London congress: principle of the centralization of the RSDWP, self-determination (Article 9 of the Program) interpreted as the right to separation, and rejection of the agrarian program, judged unsuited to Transcaucasia.[101]

Concerned as they were with acting in the Armenian environment and detaching the Armenian peasant and worker from nationalist ideology, they wanted to organize Armenian workers. In their *Manifesto* they called for the transformation of Russia into a "Federative Democratic State" in which Transcaucasia would enjoy wide autonomy.[102] They invoked the specific conditions of Transcaucasia — which is why their rivals nicknamed them "Specifists" — such as the existence of a mosaic of nationalities, the fact that the national movement had preceded the workers' movement, and the linguistic and religious cleavages within the working class. The Specifists therefore demanded that the SDAWO should be the sole representative of the Armenian proletariat and that it should be autonomous in its internal affairs. They called for the restructuring of the RSDWP on the basis of a federal organization of national SD parties. The influence of Austro-Marxism and the Bund, whose skirmishes with the *Iskra* before and after the London congress were discussed by the Caucasians, is obvious.

Better still, at the London congress, Lenin had constantly used the Caucasians against the Bund. The operation had been carefully prepared as is shown by the over-representation of the three Caucasian committees whose delegates, two Armenians (B. Gnuniantz of Baku, A. Zurabov of Batum) and one Georgian (D. Topuridze of Tiflis), received two votes each and the under-representation of the Bund which was given five votes.[103] Gnuniantz's interventions against the Bund — which Lenin had published — used the example of Transcaucasia where there existed an international organization with a territorial base, carrying on effective propaganda in three and later, with the addition of Azeri Turkish, four languages.[104] From this time onward it was as if Lenin considered Transcaucasia with its national microcosms as a laboratory in which to try out a Russian model (in opposition to the Austrian model) of internationalism: a single centralized party, using local languages (which had already become "transmission belts") for propaganda and agitation. Whether they became Bolsheviks (Shahumian, Kasian) or Mensheviks (Zurabov, Erzinkian) — the split between the "majority" and the "minority" occurred in mid-October 1903 — the Armenian Social Democrats' views were exactly the same.[105]

The Specifists, accused of being the "imitators of their Jewish and Austrian masters," did not deny this influence, but quoted the examples of the Second International, which they defined as a federation of autonomous national parties, and the Social Democratic organizations in Livonia, Poland, and Lithuania.[106] What needs emphasis here is not only the role of influences, but also the similarities among socialists from non-Russian minorities (Jews, Poles, Armenians) in quest of a realistic internationalism built on a concrete national base: "the struggle of the proletariat of one nation differs from the struggle of the proletariat of another nation as much as the expressions of their nationalism differ."[107] Finally, underlying it all, one can observe among the Specifists an admitted suspicion of a unified Social Democratic party whose centralism would perpetuate Great Russian supremacy.

Unlike the Bund which was a mass party, the SDAWO was never more than a tiny group, facing the hostility of the RSDWP and the Dashnak Party; its goal of organizing Armenian workers was never realized. Thus, the interest of Specifism lies not in the history of the movement, which was broken up by the tsarist police in 1908, but in its contribution to Armenian political thought. The Specifist intelligentsia, "these generals without an army" mocked by the Armenian Bolsheviks, was the channel for the penetration and "naturalization" of Marxism in Armenian society rather than for its spreading, for, quite unlike Georgian society, it encountered great resistance there.

In their press, *Sotsialist* (The Socialist), *Kiank* (Life), and *Dsayn* (Voice), as well as in their literature, the Specifists invented Armenian neologisms, and thus introduced a Marxist economic and political terminology.[108] In their essays, devoted to Armenian problems (history, society, literature, and international relations), their originality lay in using the method of dialectical materialism. A final point is that they sought their models in German and Austrian Marxism rather than in Russian Marxism.

The Specifists were accused of nationalism by the Armenian Social Democrats. Yet the Specifists themselves were not particularly tolerant; they were obsessed with the nationalism of the Dashnak party "besotted by the illusion of being able to settle the problem of Turkish Armenia by using the simple faith of the Caucasian proletariat of which it is the worst enemy."[109] What was needed to resolve the contradiction between the class and nation, the Specifists insisted, was a national workers' organization which, in a multinational state, was the only way to reach the proletariat of each nation effectively. Finally, the SDAWO, an organization of the Armenian proletariat in Russia, declared that it was not its role to settle the Armenian Question — an international question — whose solution had to be found by the Armenians in Turkey themselves!

Soviet historiography has so muddied the tracks that it is difficult to assess the real influence of the Social Democrats in the Caucasion Union of the RSDWP among Armenian workers. Judging from the number of titles in the Armenian-language Bolshevik press and from the number of issues published (112 issues in all between 1902 and 1914), this influence was comparable to that of the Specifists.[110] But comparisons must end there. The Social Democrats had no separate organization. They were not addressing themselves to Armenian workers in particular but to the Transcaucasian proletariat in general. They worked with Russian, Georgian, and, more rarely, Azeri Social Democrats, at the level of a factory, a town, or a region. While they stressed the need to develop a Marxist literature in the Caucasian national languages, the purpose was to be better understood. Certainly, they wrote and published in Armenian, although less than the Specifists, and they used as much if not more Russian, which tended in their mouths and under their pens to become the language of proletarian internationalism in Transcaucasia.

The Mensheviks, who left the bosom of the Union of Armenian Social Democrats with the Bolsheviks, were to remain always a tiny minority of intellectuals — Gevorg Gharadjian, Aramayis Erzinkian, Arshak Zurabov (founder of the only Armenian-language Menshevik daily, *Hosank*, and SD deputy in the Second Duma in 1906) — on the fringes of Armenian society, even in Tiflis which was at once the capital of the Armenians and the stronghold of Menshevism. The reason was that behind the language of the most intransigent internationalism, in Transcaucasia Menshevism tended increasingly to become a Georgian party, a phenomenon which revived national rivalries.

The Bolsheviks and the Armenian Question

Armenian Bolsheviks — a small core of intellectuals and workers including Suren Spandarian, Melik Melikian, and Asatur Kakhoyan — were dominated by the figure of Stepan Shahumian (1878-1918).[111] This ex-student (he had been expelled from Riga Polytechnic Institute and dropped out of the University of Berlin) became, in 1904 (the year in which he published the first Armenian edition of the *Communist Party Manifesto*), a professional revolutionary and an unconditional Leninist.[112] After 1905, he was active almost exclusively in Transcaucasia, where, similar to a number of other Caucasians such as Stalin, Ordjonikidze, and Enukidze, he became a typical revolutionary, organizer, and propagandist of the interior.

The Bolsheviks, who had a more **internationalist practice** than the Mensheviks, attracted Social Democrats from other national minorities around a Russian core and were influential between 1905 and 1907 in the regions with **heavy industry** and a **multinational proletariat** (like Baku and Allaverdi) as well as in the stations and depots where the Russian element was dominant (Alexandrapol, Kars). They had little success, though, in the Armenian provinces (Gharabagh, Zangezur, and Erevan); but, thanks to the influence of Shahumian who was very familiar with the region, their influence in Borchalu was durable.

Bolsheviks and Mensheviks waged a bitter struggle for the conquest and control of the Caucasian SD committees through 1912. But the two joined forces to combat nationalism which they always subordinated to class struggle. This pattern was particularly obvious within Armenian society.

Kayds (Spark) was the first legal organ of Armenian social democracy (47 issues between April and August 1906).[113] At the time Bolsheviks and Mensheviks were still unseparated. It was in Kayds that essays on the national question by Stalin and Shahumian challenged the Specifists with the arguments used against the Bund.[114] There was no national specificity requiring an autonomous organization of the Armenian working class: the latter would find the solution to its problems in the struggle waged with and under the leadership of the Russian proletariat; any system of federal organization in the RSDWP would mean nationalism and separatism, argued Shahumian and Stalin. Against the Dashnaks, they launched what was to become the ritual accusation of "bourgeois nationalism."

However, this line of argument did not enable the Armenian SDs to dispose of the Armenian Question. *Proletariati Krive*, the organ of the Caucasian Union, published in 1903 a letter written by Engels in 1894. While not denying the existence of an Armenian Question, Engels feared that it might serve tsarist expansionism in Asia Minor and he wrote that the fate of the oppressed peoples of Asia Minor must be linked to the fall of the autocracy.[115] This was to remain until 1917 the theory of Armenian Bolsheviks.

As for the national question, Shahumian believed that it would only be settled by a radical solution of the social question. He put forward a dialectical interpretation of the right to self-determination in the program of the RSDWP, condemned federalism outright (it raised barriers that divided proletarians), and advocated the transformation of the Russian Empire into a democratic state combining political centralism and administrative autonomy.[116]

The National Populists Adjust

Shaken by the wave of strikes that broke over Transcaucasia, faced with the labor movement and the rise of nationalism, lambasted by Marxist criticism, and sensing the approach of a Russian revolution, the Hunchak and Dashnak parties were forced to revise tactics and strategy from 1903 onward.

Once again, it was the Caucasian Hunchaks who were the first to demonstrate their sensitivity to the "New Word" (*Nove Slovo*), and the "New Task" (freeing the Armenian working class) as opposed to the "Old" and "Sacred Task" of freeing the Armenian nation.

A third Hunchakian congress in London (September 1901 to March 1902) had theoretically rebuilt, on the remains of the Hunchak Center and the Verakazmial party, a unified Hunchakian party, a unified Center, and a Provisional Executive Committee. But despite the call for the "total fraternity of Armenian revolutionaries," the two factions had retained their respective programs and had only united momentarily against Avetis Nazarbekian. In fact, the factional struggles deepened to the point where they resulted in a series of fratricidal outrages in the United States, London, the Balkans, and the Caucasus before, during, and after the fourth congress. It was between the fourth and the fifth congresses, held respectively in London in September 1903 and in Paris in September 1905, that the controversy developed over the need for a revision, on truly socialist and Marxist bases, of Hunchak party strategy.[117]

Led by Avetis Nazarbekian, Ruben Khan Azat, Sarkis Kasian, Grigor Vardanian, and Ahriman (all Caucasians) the left wing campaigned in *Veradsnutiun* and then *Abaka* (Future), organs devoted to the analysis of the problems of socialism in Armenian life.[118] These writers stressed the teleological role of Armenian workers and showed that Armenian emancipation would result from a Pan-Russian revolution, which was the Bolshevik thesis. They proposed to struggle on two fronts which required a division in the party: in the Caucasus and in Russia the Hunchakian SD party would enter the RSDWP; in the Ottoman Empire, it would exist as an autonomous party on the sole basis of a program for the freedom of Armenians in Turkey.

After fierce debates, the fifth congress rejected the proposals of the Caucasian intelligentsia to forget the Armenian Question and concentrate all efforts in the Russian Empire. It reasserted the unity of the party by deciding to have "a proletarian revolutionary activity in the Caucasus and to struggle to establish a political democracy on Marxist principles in Turkey." But the victory of the supporters of the "Old Oath" led by an Armenian from Turkey, Sabah-Gulian, could not prevent a new split.

When the "Nazarbekists" returned to the Caucasus, they rejected the decisions of the congress and decided to merge with the RSDWP. Some, such as Nazarbekian and Khan Azat, followed Martov's advice to accept the RSDWP program, to join no faction, and to await the unification of the Bolsheviks and the Mensheviks.[119] Others joined singly or brought whole sections (such as Erevan and Baku) over to the Bolsheviks, breaking up the Hunchak workers' organizations which had been extremely combative during the famous Baku strike of December 1904. The demoralized Caucasian Hunchaks survived in a few moribund branches. The revolutionary crisis had brought starkly to the fore the contradictions between the Russian workers' movement and the Armenian Question. It also led to the transfer of the Hunchak party leadership into the hands of Armenians in Turkey. Without abandoning socialist language, the Hunchak party became centered in the United States, Egypt, and the Ottoman Empire. However, the party remained without impact on Ottoman events until the Young Turk Revolution.

At the beginning of the twentieth century, the Dashnak party was wholly taken up with problems of organizing — without class struggle and without socialism — Armenians in the Ottoman, Russian, and Persian Empires as well as in the Diaspora. The problems of propaganda among socialist parties in the International also concerned them.

In the Russian Empire, it had established networks, including Armenian workers, but did not carry on any activity against the autocracy. The activities of the *Potorik* (Storm) group, established in Filibe (Bulgaria) in 1901, cannot be considered such.[120] It was given the task of topping up the party's coffers and collecting from the Caucasian Armenian bourgeoisie "the tax for the freedom of the Fatherland" on threat of death ("internal economic terrorism").

It was tsarist policy that, by arousing the unanimous resistance of Armenians, brought the Dashnak party back to life and drove it to adopt defensive tactics (Central Self-Defense Committee) and then the armed offensive against the Russian government. The party did not take this course without hesitation. This is demonstrated best by the behavior of a group of Caucasian *fedayees* who were sent to the relief of Sasun, surrounded by the Turkish army during the summer of 1904. When surprised on the frontier at Olti by Russian Cossacks, they let themselves be massacred by the Russians without firing a shot.

The period from the summer of 1903 to the summer of 1905 was a vital one in the history of the Dashnak party. Its center of gravity moved to Transcaucasia, where it rapidly gained influence among Armenians as a whole. Its ranks swelled as the idea spread among militants that the party was struggling not merely for the freedom of Armenians in Turkey but for that of the whole nation. The third Dashnak congress, which was held in Sofia (February-March 1904) marked this turning point.[122] It strengthened the executive (Council of the ARF), again gave priority to actions in the Ottoman Empire (organization of Cilicia, assassination of Sultan Abdul Hamid), but it also decided to "assume the self-defense of the Armeno-Caucasian element" by propaganda, terror, demonstrations, and armed resistance.[123] It authorized Dashnak workers to participate in strikes, but it intended to keep them on a tight leash.

During 1904, the party embarked on terrorism against "traitors" and the bureaucracy, and boycotted the Russian administration by creating schools, courts, and even prisons (Kars) in the Armenian regions. It emerged at last from its political isolation in Russia and participated in the November 1904 Paris conference that brought together nine movements including liberals, Social-Revolutionaries, Polish socialists, Georgian federalists, and others; the conference's decisions (the overthrow of the autocratic regime and self-determination of nations) were approved by the fourth Dashnak regional congress in December 1904.[124] This same congress recorded the party's progress in the Caucasus: 121 groups in Kars, 265 in Baku and its suburbs, 161 in Alexandrapol, 82 in Batum, 24 in Shushi, 240 in the villages of Gharabagh, 30 in Tiflis, 2 in Erevan, and 31 in the northern Caucasus.[125] This impressive listing shows that the Dashnak party had become a national and popular organization that included workers in Baku, peasants in Gharabagh, and the petty bourgeois in Tiflis (stronghold of both the liberal and the conservative Armenian bourgeoisie). One exception raises a problem: the case of Erevan.

The First Revolution and Ethnic Conflict

The 1905 Revolution led to a climate of unusual violence in Transcaucasia: there was wave upon wave of peasant uprisings as well as strikes and uprisings by railway workers, office workers, artisans, and secondary school students. Until the end of 1907, the authorities were powerless to deal with the attacks, expropriations, kidnappings, and banditry. The revolt of the nationalities rapidly became complicated by the conflict among the nationalities themselves.

As early as February 1905, a few days after Red Sunday, a serious clash between Tatars and Armenians occurred in Baku. The clash spread to towns and villages in eastern and central Transcaucasia where the two ethnic groups lived side by side.[126] This "Armeno-Tatar war," begun as a pogrom of Armenians, took all the revolutionaries by surprise. The latter interpreted it, universally, as a diversionary maneuver launched by the autocracy against the multinational army of the Caucasian proletariat. In a few weeks, Armenian capitalists, workers, and peasants as well as their property were threatened by the Muslim population.

Perhaps following the example of the Bund organizing self-defense units in 1902 and certainly inspired by the *fedayee* movement, the Dashnak party became heavily involved in the self-defense of the Armenian community. In the name of national solidarity and armed resistance, it imposed contributions on rich and poor alike; it formed mobile units led by *fedayees* who fell back into Turkey or by local militants (Nikol Duman, Vardan, Gulkhandian, Dro, Hamazasp, Khecho, Sako, Arakel, Murat, Avo, Keri, among others); it rushed to the aid of threatened districts; it drew up a plan for urban guerrilla warfare; it trained terrorist squads (execution of Governor-General Nakashidze); and it oversaw the flood of men and money.[127] In the space of a few months, the Dashnaktsutiun became the dominant party in the Armenian community in the Caucasus and it imposed itself on the community as an authoritarian arbiter.

But the arming of Armenians was soon followed by the arming of Muslims. In a cycle of atrocious reprisals and counter-reprisals,[128] the Armeno-Tatar war lasted until the spring of 1906, distracting the Armenians and Tatars from their revolutionary tasks, according to the SDs.

The Specifists as well as the Georgian and Armenian SDs turned against the Dashnak party. They accused it of being manipulated by the Russian bureaucracy, inflaming racial and religious hatreds, stifling class consciousness under nationalism and racism, breaking the unity of the Caucasian revolutionary movement, and filling its coffers by defending the oil wells and factories belonging to the Armenian bourgeoisie.

The Armenian Bolsheviks, who were quite numerous in the Baku Committee, were anxious to win over the large Muslim proletariat in the town; they totally condemned self-defense and, envisaging the fraternal union of Turkish and Armenian proletarians, created the *Koč-Devet* (Call) — a bilingual (Armenian-Turkish) organ of the Armenian section of the Baku and Hummet Committee (May-July 1906).[129] The Specifists, seeing the enormous fire in the Armenian oil wells (August 1905) as an act that deprived the Armenian proletariat of its work, sought to break the Dashnak military monopoly by arming the Armenian workers.[130]

In June 1905, the Dashnak party's "Caucasian Project" (*Kovkasian Nakhagids*) was the response to these criticisms, to the SD successes in Baku and Tiflis, and to the internal tensions that were tearing the party apart.[131] The statement was the work of the Council of the ARF and was prefaced by a wordy preamble ("a Marxist and SD mish-mash").[132] It laid down a new line of action in the Caucasus. The Dashnaktsutiun defined itself as a "popular party," defending "the point of view, and the political and economic interests of the mass of workers." The party declared that it was struggling against the autocracy in the Pan-Russian movement and recognized the class struggle as well as the need to extend the political revolution by a socialist revolution. It demanded the transformation of Transcaucasia into a democratic federative republic on the basis of the widest local autonomy and a series of measures ranging from the eight-hour day to the gradual collectivization of land. Because of the novelty of its socialist content, the project had the effect of a bomb: it was keenly discussed, criticized or praised, but it remained a dead letter.

The intensification of the Armeno-Tatar war in Baku and the defense of the Armenian community mobilized the Dashnak forces. Taking advantage of the general anarchy in the Caucasus, the party became a sort of "national state" with its own army, police, courts, arsenals, and war chest. Its opponents had an easy time denouncing the development of this "repressive apparatus."

However, by the end of 1905 difficulties were already appearing. The Armenian bourgeoisie, first driven by fear into the arms of the Dashnaks (it secured protection of its life and property in return for contributions to the party's coffers), was reassured by the restoration of the Armenian clergy's property and by the October Manifesto which adopted an overtly hostile attitude toward the Dashnaks. Armenian liberals, some of whom joined the ranks of the Constitutional Democratic or KD party, distanced themselves from a party whose aims and methods they found repugnant: *Mshak* and *Murdj* (Hammer) became sharply anti-Dashnak from 1907 onward.[133] The militarization of the party created a category of "party soldiers" who were hostile to socialism and undisciplined. The increase in party membership and its sociological transformations (massive entry of the middle classes) led some militants to wonder about its nature. Was the Dashnaktsutiun a national party or a revolutionary class party? Was its aim to free Armenians in Turkey or to lead Armenian society everywhere? What should be its tactics toward the Caucasian and Pan-Russian revolutionary movement? What tactics should it adopt to achieve the freedom of Armenians in Turkey?

The Dashnaktsutiun Threatened

It was around these questions that, during the spring of 1906, a double internal opposition began to take shape: on the right, that of the "Mihranakans" and on the left, that of the "Young Dashnaks."

The Mihranakans, who were supported by the *fedayees* and had widespread sympathy in Turkey, refused to become involved in Caucasian affairs and socialism once the Tatar danger had disappeared. They sought to bring the party back to its Ottoman aims alone.[134] But the Mihranakan opposition, compromised by the support given it by the Caucasian bourgeoisie which was all too keen to see the Dashnaks go back to Asia Minor, was quickly liquidated.

The Young Dashnaks, a small minority of Caucasian socialist intellectuals, did not accept that the party should identify itself with the nation and that "exploiters and exploited should militate side by side in its ranks."[135] Their theoretician, Mravian (Arsen Amirian), the future Bolshevik Commissar in Baku in 1918, criticized Dashnak tactics.[136] The party must transfer the major part of its forces to the Caucasus, purge its ranks of opportunist elements, and seek an alliance with revolutionary parties in Russia, since the "victorious Russian revolution will have the same influence on the destiny of neighboring countries, including Turkey and Persia, as the French Revolution . . . the liberation of Turkish Armenia will result from . . ." that of Russia. Levon Atabekian (Rikhard) demonstrated through socialism that it was impossible to link the two causes of Armenians in Turkey (where socialism remained a utopia) and Armenians in Russia.[137] The Young Dashnaks split away and "separated" themselves off in order to militate among the SR or, more rarely, among the SD. The issues they raised obliged the party to revise its tactics and strategy.

The fourth congress in Vienna (February-May 1907), one of the most important in the history of the Dashnak party, cut through the contradictions and preserved its unity.[138] It adopted a socialist program, but gave a special place to national problems by stressing the complexity of the class struggle in countries where a dominant nation and oppressed minorities existed side by side. It insisted on the struggle of workers of oppressed nations for their national culture as the vital instrument of their progress and asserted that nations would survive in the future socialist society.

The new program, inspired by the SR example, recognized the differences across the border and proposed different aims. For Turkish Armenia the program demanded political democracy based on local autonomy and federative links within the Ottoman Empire. For Russian Armenia, it demanded a democratic Transcaucasian republic with wide local autonomy integrated into a Russian federated republic. The common demands related to the separation of Church and State, popular militias, the socialization of land, the nationalization of the mines, progressive income tax, the development of cooperatives, workers' control, and the eight-hour day.

Faced with choosing between the Caucasian worker and the Anatolian peasant, the Dashnak party in 1907 manifested a considerable capacity to adapt. But this should not obscure the fact that the two-fold program implicitly accepted the failure of the "Bulgarian way" and abandoned the possible future reunification of Armenians. Finally, in the same year, the Dashnak party adopted (along with the SR, Jewish SERP, Georgian Socialist federalists, and so on) the principle of extra-territorial cultural autonomy.[139] It received the stamp of approval as a socialist party, despite the violent hostility of the Caucasian SDs, by joining the Second International at the Stuttgart congress.[140]

This socialist stamp of approval sealed the efforts of the Caucasian Dashnaks — in particular those of Mikayel Varandian[141] — who had been seeking since 1900 to use the International as a tribune for the Armenian Question and had alerted the International Socialist Bureau (ISB) in 1905 over the "second Kishinev" that was occurring in Baku.[142] It did not remove the conviction held by Armenian, Georgian, and Russian Marxists that Dashnaks were using socialism for purely nationalist ends. The SR, whose program and tactics had inspired the Dashnak program of 1907, continued always to show a scornful skepticism toward the socialism of their partners. In short, while Dashnaks won support among some democrats and socialists in Western Europe, they did not allay the hostility of the Caucasian SDs.

Socialism Dominant

What is striking is the amount of socialist oneupmanship in which all the revolutionary parties engaged in this rising phase of Transcaucasian national movements.[143] The development in the Georgian national movement of an intransigent ("intolerant") Menshevism, which bore the mark of ideology or the bane of scientific socialism, is related to the fact that, of all the Transcaucasian societies, Georgian society was the most rural, the most "feudal," and the least affected by industrial and urban changes.[144] But Dashnak socialism was neither Marxist, scientific, nor ideological. The articles, pamphlets, and works of Dashnak theoreticians like Mikayel Varandian, Eghishe Topchian, Shahkhatuni, Ruben Darbinian, Garegin Khajak, Rostom, Zardarian, and Ervant Frankian as well as the choice of socialist texts translated and published by the Dashnaks reveal a great eclecticism. Dashnak socialism was a composite doctrine in which there coexisted side by side an old base of Russian populism (Mikhailovski) and Italian pre-Marxist socialism (Mazzini, Garibaldi) mixed with some elements drawn from Marx and his German followers, both orthodox (Kautsky) and revisionist (Bernstein). After 1907, Dashnak socialism modeled itself more and more on the socialism of Jaurès — an idealistic and generous doctrine, aspiring to justice, democracy, and freedoms that would be respectful of the nations and fatherlands. This doctrine finally convinced the Dashnaks that socialism was a means of defense against national oppression more than an inevitable stage in economic development.

At the beginning of the century social stratification was quite developed among Caucasian Armenians, whereas it had hardly begun among the Armenians in the Ottoman Empire. In the space of a few years, from 1902 to 1907, in the small world of the Armenians in the Caucasus the policy of Russification, the workers' movement, and the 1905 Revolution had brought out the contradictions between the class struggle in the Caucasus and the struggles for national emancipation in the Ottoman Empire; these events shook the Pan-Armenian revolutionary parties (both Hunchak and Dashnak), and demanded clear replies from them. They had driven a section of Young Armenians, ideologized through the medium of Russian culture, to become activists in one of the great SD or SR Pan-Russian revolutionary organizations. Everywhere new events had provoked a search for "new ways" to find a solution to the obsessive national problem.[145] Hunchaks, Dashnaks, Bolsheviks, Mensheviks, Specifists, and Armenian SRs gave every reply made possible by the combination and ordering of the concepts of class and nation (the **nation** being ephemeral for the Marxists and absolute for the Dashnaks). The revolutionary struggles and the party struggles during the election campaigns for the first three Dumas led to the appearance in the Caucasus of an Armenian political class, from which were to emerge the personnel of the Republic of Armenia (1918-1920) and of Soviet Armenia in the 1920s.

The Dashnak party, whose socialism was the least radical and whose nationalism was the most marked, barred the road to Marxism and tended to become a dominant party among Armenians at the very time when Menshevism was enjoying the same destiny among Georgians. After 1912, the *Musavat* (Equality) party, whose leaders turned toward a Turkey rejuvenated by the Young Turk Revolution, became dominant among the Azeris.

The divergent political development of the three Transcaucasian national movements, none of which was separatist, inflamed national rivalries. Because geography had placed them in the middle of Transcaucasia, because history had scattered them among Georgian and Azeri populations, and because Armenian city-dwellers were concentrated in Tiflis and Baku, Armenians united their neighbors against them.

Georgian national hostility was hidden behind socialist rivalries between Mensheviks and Dashnaks; the Armeno-Tatar war acted as a catalyst for Azeri national feeling which from Shushi to Baku developed as much, if not more, against the Armenians as against the Russians. For the fact was that in the Transcaucasian environment both religious and cultural separation (Muslims/Christians) and reciprocal prejudices based on centuries of Muslim domination existed. There the speed of social development among Armenians had created conditions — visible domination over a number of sectors of the surrounding society (industry, finance, and trade), more rapid upward social mobility, and attraction toward extremist ideological currents — which strengthened the negative attitudes of Muslims toward them.

4
"THE STOLYPIN REACTION" AND THE REVOLUTIONS IN THE EAST (1908-1912)

From 1908 onward, the ebbing of the tide of revolution and the waning of political life, which were manifest in every region in the Empire, were even more marked in Transcaucasia where order had at last been restored. But while Russian industry underwent rapid growth, the Baku oil industry failed to recover the leading position it had enjoyed in the world at the beginning of the century. In Baku, the decline in the number of strikes (from June 1908 to July 1913) and the abandonment by workers in the oil industry of the two great trade unions, control of which was fought over by Mensheviks, Bolsheviks, and even Dashnaks, were both evidence of the regression of the workers' movement.[146]

A New Repression

The "Stolypin reaction" took the form of harsh repression (executions, arrests, and deportations); in the Caucasus it affected revolutionary parties of all nationalities. The small organizations, which had neither the militants, the funds, nor the press of the big parties, were broken up. The Armenian specifist organization disappeared; a few Hunchak committees survived from Batum to Baku.[147] The Armenian Mensheviks and the SRs lived twilight hours in Tiflis and Baku. Those Bolsheviks who had not been arrested withdrew to Baku. The combined efforts of Shahumian, Spandarian, and Stalin made it one of the few strongholds of Leninism during these years, but the Armenian-language social democratic press, of whatever tendency, disappeared almost entirely.[148]

The Dashnak party, whose international structure (it took the shape of a Diaspora that already stretched from Persia to the United States) as well as terrorist and defensive actions had led the tsarist bureaucracy to overestimate its power in terms of membership, money, weapons, and influence, was dealt with severely. Some militants and leaders, who were too deeply involved, had to flee. The arrest of hundreds of other Dashnaks was the occasion for a vast trial, whose investigation in St. Petersburg took several years and ended in a docket 20,000 pages long.[149] In early 1912, the 55 accused received quite light sentences, less because of the skill of some of their lawyers such as Kerensky and Miliukov than because the tsarist government was anxious to win over Armenian public opinion at a time when it was beginning to pursue an active policy in the Ottoman Empire. From 1908 to 1912 the number of Caucasian militants belonging to the Dashnak party, already reduced by the purges and the crisis of 1906-1907, was reduced again. However, its organizations continued to exist in semi-clandestinity. The party did not carry out any more revolutionary operations in Transcaucasia; but it developed its cultural activities, won over a section of the intellectuals, and managed to keep a legal daily, *Horizon*, in Tiflis.[150] In terms of its circulation (10,000 to 11,000 copies) and its quality, the *Horizon* rivaled *Mshak*. In this way the party retained its hold over the popular and middle classes of Armeno-Caucasian society, whose unitary national consciousness it helped to forge and whose attention it again redirected toward the Armenians in Turkey when socialism was suffering an eclipse in Russia.

New Revolutions

Since the summer of 1908, the center of gravity of the Armenian movement, and particularly of the Dashnak party, had moved from the Caucasus to the Ottoman and Persian empires. The "Stolypin reaction," which had forced Caucasian, Azeri, Georgian, and Armenian activists to stop their activities or to flee, coincided with other revolutions that opened up a new field of action for them: the Tabriz revolt and the second revolutionary wave of the Persian constitutional movement (June 1908) as well as the Young Turk Revolution and the restoration of the Ottoman constitution (July 1908).

From 1908 to 1912, this chapter in the history of the Armenian revolutionary movement finds Armenians of the Caucasus rushing to Constantinople, Van, Erzerum, Tabriz, Resht, and Teheran. SDs, Hunchaks, and Dashnaks, isolated or organized, played a significant role that is too rich and too complex to be dealt with completely here. In general, though, the tactical and strategic changes made by the Dashnak party which, by virtue of the scale of its organization in the Ottoman Empire and in Iranian Azerbaidjan (an area that had been organized into a revolutionary base for the *fedayee* movement since the 1890s), out-classed all its rivals.[151]

The Dashnaks learned lessons from the deadlock in the Armenian Question, from the Russian revolutionary experience, and from criticisms made by the Specifists and the Young Dashnaks against the sterility of the "Bulgarian way;"[152] they observed the decline of the Armenian population in the vilayets of Anatolia; and they took careful note of the awakening of the Muslim peoples (market disturbances at Van, Erzerum, Kastemoni in 1906[153] and the *andjumans* movement in Persia).[154] They, therefore, became convinced that Ottoman despotism could only be overthrown by the combined action of all the peoples in the Empire. Hence they sought an alliance with Turkish, Azeri, and Persian Muslim reformists and revolutionaries to democratize and to modernize the ancient states of the East. Finally, oppressed by despotic empires, which were themselves victims of the economic and even political imperialism of the Western

Powers, Armenians came to appreciate the tensions between capitalism and traditional societies as well as between imperialism and the resistance to imperialism which the Persian constitutional movement and the Young Turk movement represented.

Socialism — of which they were, in varying degrees, the pioneers in the East — enabled them to settle, at least in theory, the contradictions between the demands of Muslim nationalism (independence, economic and cultural progress) and its reactionary features (xenophobia, rejection of Western values, Islamic fundamentalism), and then to propose a democratic and peaceful co-existence of all the peoples in the East.

This new policy, prepared by the dual program of the Vienna congress (1907), was approved by the Congress of Opposition Parties in the Ottoman Empire organized in Paris during December 1907 on the initiative of the Dashnak party and its representative, the Caucasian Aknuni.[155] In July 1908, from Constantinople to Mush and Van, Dashnaks came out into the open as the allies of the Committee of Union and Progress and laid down their arms. From 1908 to 1912, despite the profound split precipitated by the Adana massacres (March-April 1909) and the increasingly strong feelings that the policy of Turkification, centralization, and the absence of real reforms (agrarian, administrative, and judicial) in Anatolia were linked to the massacres, they remained faithful to the line of Ottomanism but retained the specifically national form of their organization.[156]

In Persia, the Caucasians in every Armenian organization (Hunchak and Dashnak *fedayees* in Tabriz, Resht, and Teheran, Social Democrats in Tabriz, and Hunchaks in Enzeli) rushed to help the Azeri and Persian patriots and provided them with theoretical or practical help.[157] The Dashnak party, whose prestige was enormous both on account of its Caucasian military exploits reported by the Persian workers in Baku and for its links with the Second International, threw itself from 1909 onward into the struggle of Persian democrats against the Qajar monarchy and Russian imperialism. Organized by Rostom and led by Nikol Duman and Keri, the Dashnak *fedayees* placed at the service of the revolting *andjumans* in Tabriz (1908-1909) their knowledge as bomb-makers, weapons experts, and strategists. Eprem Khan, a survivor of the Kukunian expedition and Siberian prisons as well as a real Dashnak adventurer nicknamed the "Armenian Garibaldi," seized Teheran (July 1909) with the Bakhtiars and restored the constitution. After three years of guerrilla war against the "monarchists," he met his death just when the intervention of the Russian army put an end to the Constitutional Movement (1912).[158] For, after crushing defeats in the Far East, Russia reappeared in the Near East, with a plan for the partition of Persia into zones of influence (1907), the determination to struggle against German expansionism, and the project to build the Anatolian railways.

The Revolution Foiled?

In Transcaucasia, the skillful policy of Viceroy Vorontsov-Dashknov reconciled the Church and the Armenian bourgeoisie with the Russian government.[159] The restoration of internal order freed the bourgeoisie of the unwanted Dashnak tutelage and the ebbing of the revolutionary tide restored it to its place as a "ruling class" in the municipal Dumas as well as in the state Duma.[160] Finally, the Armeno-Tatar war once again convinced the party that against the "Turkish threat" on both sides of the frontier, Armenians needed Russian protection. Its patriotism, fueled by the tale of the misfortunes of Anatolian Armenians, and its loyalty to Russia served as the basis for Russian diplomacy which suddenly resurrected the Armenian Question during the First Balkan War. In the autumn of 1912, Catholicos Gevork V was authorized to present Tsar Nicholas II with a request for protection and reforms on behalf of Armenians in Turkey. The Dashnaks did not have the initiative in Tiflis, where the reappearance of an Armenian National Bureau sealed the new alliance between the Caucasian bourgeoisie and the tsarist government; they did not have it in Constantinople, where the Patriarch and the National Assembly — disappointed by the failures of Ottomanism and submerged by requests from Anatolia — threw themselves wholeheartedly behind the new policy; nor did they have it in Paris, where Boghos Nubar Pasha had been delegated by the Catholicos. They were consulted and associated but they were a minority in these new centers of the national movement.

The return to the "diplomatic way" advocated by Armenian ruling circles since 1878 signified a policy of intervention, placed under the auspices of Russian imperialism just when the Balkan crisis was weakening the Ottoman Empire and exacerbating Turkish nationalism. It was a denial of the "revolutionary way" in which nationalism and socialism had co-existed. The rallying of the Dashnaks, in particular of the Caucasian Dashnaks, was part of an outburst of Armenian nationalism which was to show itself to be dangerously ignorant of Turkish realities.[161]

NOTES

[1]1375: end of Cilician Armenia.

[2]In the eighteenth century, Armenian merchants in New Julfa sought to create an Armenian cultural center in the West. From the sixteenth to the nineteenth centuries, the Catholicos and the bishops drew up plans for crusades led by the Pope and the Christian states against Islam.

[3]*Ermeni Millet* ("Armenian community"), organized under the leadership of the Armenian Patriarchate of Constantinople in the fifteenth century. Through the *polozhenye*, the Russian government in 1836 guaranteed the Armenian Apostolic Church a number of rights, particularly in the field of education.

[4]*Azdarar* (Monitor), the first Armenian journal (published beginning in 1794 in Madras), expressed the patriotic and even republican aspirations of a small but wealthy community of merchants whose goal was the independence of Armenia.

[5]Such was the meaning of the famous "Appeal to the Armenian nation" by the Archbishop of Tiflis Nerses Ashtareketsi (1770-1857). V.A. Parsamian, *Hay zhoghovurdi patmutiun* [History of the Armenian People] (Erevan, 1967), Vol. III, p. 64.

[6]March 16, 1921: treaty between Turkey and Soviet Russia, which settled the frontier problems between Transcaucasia and Turkey.

[7]The overall figures and the percentages for the Armenian population of Turkey are only approximate.

[8]V.A. Parsamian, *op. cit.*, p. 272.

[9] Except for the *melik* of Gharabagh and a few "princes" in Sasun and Zeytun. An administrative nobility finally appeared in Russia during the nineteenth century.

[10] Historic Armenia stretched from eastern Anatolia to the governorate of Erevan and Iranian Aderbadakan (Azerbaijan).

[11] K. Kévonian, "Marchands arméniens au XVIIe siècle," *Cahiers du monde russe et soviétique* (Paris), 2 (1975):199-244.

[12] The existence of powerful *amiras* in Constantinople should be noted. H. Barsoumian, "Economic Role of the Armenian Amira Class in the Ottoman Empire," *Armenian Review* (Boston), 3(1979):310-316.

[13] A. Ter Minassian, "Aux origines du marxisme arménien: les spécifistes," *Cahiers du monde russe et soviétique* (Paris), 1-2(1978):72.

[14] A lengthy debate developed over the term "temporary migrants" in the Dashnak press and *Mshak*, the liberal paper, from 1903 onward.

[15] This was observable in Constantinople as well as in Tiflis during the mid-nineteenth century.

[16] For the Armenian Question, see Arthur Beylérian, "Aux origines de la question arménienne du traité de San Stéfano au Congrés de Berlin (1878)," *Revue d'Histoire Diplomatique* (Paris), 1-2 (1973):1-33.

[17] National Assembly set up in 1860, National Constitution granted in 1863; on the ambiguity of the word constitution which was never used by the Ottoman authorities, see M.K. Krikorian, *Armenians in the Service of the Ottoman Empire* (London, 1978), pp. 3-5.

[18] These themes, which recur in Armenian political writing, are illustrated by concrete examples as the result of a survey in the villages around Erzerum by the newspaper *Haradj* (Forward) from 1909 onward.

[19] H., Ghazarian, *Arevmtahayeri sotsial-tntesakan ev kaghakakan katsutiune 1800-1870* [The Socioeconomic and Political Condition of the Western Armenians 1800-1870] (Erevan, 1967), pp. 412-436.

[20] A. Bennigsen, "Un témoignage sur Chamil et les guerres du Caucase," *Cahiers du monde russe et soviétique* (Paris), 2-3(1966):311-322.

[21] The problem of the relations between Kurds and Armenians was one of the major aspects of the Armenian Question. The Kurdish tribes, which had been semi-independent until the beginning of the nineteenth century, came under the control of the Ottoman bureaucracy in the second half of the nineteenth century and were used in frontier policing from 1891 onward (*Hamidiye* cavalry). Relations between Kurds and Armenians continued to go from bad to worse at the very time when Armenian revolutionaries were seeking an alliance with them.

[22] On this whole question, see V.A. Parsamian, *op. cit.*

[23] "*Millet-i-Sadika*," in contrast to the Greeks and Slavs in the Empire.

[24] See A. Beylerian, *op. cit.*, pp. 31-32

[25] Louise Nalbandian, *The Armenian Revolutionary Movement* (Berkeley, 1967).

[26] Vartan Gregorian, "The Impact of Russia on the Armenians and Armenia," in W. Vucinich (ed), *Russia and Asia* (Stanford, 1972), pp. 167-218.

[27] Founded in Tiflis during 1825 by Archbishop Nerses Ashtaraketsi. In theory it was a seminary, a fact that enabled it to survive the successive closures of Armenian schools for almost a century.

[28] Founded in 1874. Acted as an Armenian institute of higher education.

[29] It was initially a secondary school founded in 1814 by the Lazarev family, a powerful family of Armenian industrialists in Moscow. Opened during 1815, in 1827 it became the Lazarev Armenian Institute of Oriental Languages and played an outstanding role in the history of Armenian culture.

[30] Until 1903 nationalist ideas were predominant. Between 1903 and 1907 Marxist ideas began to gain ground. These schools were the scene of student agitation during the 1905 Revolution.

[31] The term "Asiatic darkness" was found in the writings of Hunchaks, Dashnaks, and SDs alike. This term contrasted with Western Enlightenment and Progress, implied a condemnation of the civilization of the Islamic East.

[32] This was the title of the famous work of the Specifist D. Ananun, *Rusahayeri hasarakakan zargatsume* [The Social Development of the Russian Armenians] Vol. I (Baku, 1916); Vol. II (Etchmiadzin, 1922); Vol. III (Venice, 1926).

[33] One aspect of the Russification policy under Alexander III and Nicholas II. See E. Aknuni, *Les Plaies du Caucase* (Geneva, 1905), pp. 12 et passim.

[34] V. Gregorian, *art. cit.*, pp. 197-198.

[35] The founders were Avetis Nazarbekian, Maro Vardanian (wife of Nazarbekian), Gabriel Kafian, Gevork Gharadjian (Archomedes), Ruben Khanazatian (R. Khan-Azat), and M. Manuelian.

[36] Adjective formed from *Mshak* (Cultivator), the title of an important Armenian periodical published in Tiflis from 1872 to 1921. Under the editorship of its founder Grigor Ardsruni from 1872 to 1892, *Mshak* was the spokesman of progressive and liberal Armenian patriots and extremely influential in Armenian society.

[37] R. Khan Azat, "Hai heghapokhakani husherits" [Of the Memoirs of an Armenian Revolutionary], *Hairenik Amsagir* (Boston), June 1927-May 1929.

[38] *Hunchak* (Bell) (Geneva), no. 11-12, 1888.

[39] Anarchist journal *Hamaynk* (Commune) published in London during 1894. Anarchist publications in Armenian in Paris from 1893 through 1894 consisted of translations of pamphlets by Kropotkin, E. Reclus, Jean Grave, and so on.

[40] *Hunchak* (1887-1914); *Gaghapar* (1893-1894); *Aptak* (1896-1897).

[41] In *Gaghapar* (Athens), no. 2, 1894.

[42] See details in *Patmutiun S.D. Huntchakian Kusaktsutian — 1887-1962* [History of the Hunchakian SD party — 1887-1962] (Beirut, 1962), Vol. I, (henceforward cited as PSDHK); L. Nalbandian, *op. cit.*, pp. 117-127.

[43] It seems that the boldness of Armenians who were demonstrating in the streets of the Ottoman capital convinced some of the founders of the Young Turk movement, such as Ahmed Riza, of the need to step up the struggle against the regime of Abdul Hamid so as to speed up the reforms that were necessary for the preservation of the Empire. C.J.Walker, "From Sasun to the Ottoman Bank: Turkish Armenians in the Mid-1890s," *Armenian Review*, 3(1979).

[44] M. Varandian, *Hay heghapokhakan Dashnaktsutian Patmutiun* [History of the Armenian Revolutionary Federation] (Paris, 1932), Vol. I, p. 59 (henceforward cited as *HHDP*).

[45] Manifesto of the ARF (1890) in *Divan HHDP* (Archives of the ARF), Boston, 1934, Vol. I, pp. 98-99.

[46] *Droshak* was a monthly published by the Western Bureau (one of the two offices of the Dashnak party) in European cities from 1891 to 1930.

[47] Kristapor Mikayelian (1859-1905); Rostom (Stepan Zorian) (1867-1919); Simon Zavarian (1866-1913); M. Varandian, *HHDP*, Vol. I, pp. 120-121.

[48] For the manifesto and the program of 1892, see *Divan, op, cit.*, pp. 95-102.

[49] B. Ishkhanian, *Tadjkahay khendire ev midjazgayin diplomatian* [The Question of Turkish Armenia and International Diplomacy] (Tiflis, 1906), p. 11.

[50] Kristapor Mikayelian, *Ambokhayin dramabanutiun* [The Logic of the Mobs] (1899), pp. 37-42; new ed., Beirut, n.d.

[51] B. Ishkhanian, *op. cit.*, p. 127.

[52] A. Ter Minassian, *art. cit.*, p. 87.

[53] R. Luxemburg, "The National Struggles in Turkey and Social Democracy," *Sächisiche Arbeiterzeitung*, nos. 234, 235, 235, in *Gesammelte Werke*, Berlin, 1970.

[54] *Pro Armenia*, published in Paris from 1900 to 1908, then from 1912 to 1914 with the title *Pour les peuples d'Orient*.

[55] G. Haupt, *Bureau Socialiste International*, Paris, 1909, pp. 34-36.

[56] This viewpoint was developed in the article by Ruben Tarbinian, "H.H. Dashnaktsutiun ev anor kaghakakanutiun Tiurkiayi medj" [The ARF and its policy in Turkey], *Azatamart* (Fight for freedom) (Constantinople, 1910), nos. 448-468 (irregularly).

[57] Reading the later works of the Dashnak ideologists — M. Varandian, E. Frankian, etc. — is enough to convince one on this point.

[58] Kristapor Mikayelian, "Memoirs," *Hayrenik Amsagir* (Boston), 10(1927).

[59] Raffi (1835-1888). See L. Nalbandian, *op. cit.*, pp. 57-66.

[60] It was Mkrtich Khrimian (1821-1907), nicknamed Khrimian Hayrik (Father Khrimian), successively journalist, bishop of Van, Patriarch of Constantinople, delegate to the Congress of Berlin, and Catholicos, who founded the myth of the *Erkir*; he left Constantinople in 1857 to settle in the monastery at Varag, near Van, and then that of Surb Karapet above Mush, which he revived and turned into patriotic and cultural centers.

[61] Noi Zhordania, *My Life* (California, 1968). See preface by L. Haimson, pp. v-xiv.

[62] Letter from Dastakian of the Tiflis Committee to Kristapor. Kristapor Mikayelian, *art. cit.*

[63] M. Varandian, *HHDP*, Vol. I, pp. 47-59; A. Gulkhandanian, *Hayrenik Amsagir*, 11(1940):65-71.

[64] It came from the "Union of Patriots," translated and published in Russian in no. 10-11 of *Narodnaya Volya*, cited by V. Minakhorian in *Vem* [Stone] (Paris), 3(1934):98-100.

[65] Sarkis Kukunian (1866-1913). On the psychology and fate of Kukunian and his companions: *Divan*, *op. cit.*, pp. 10-86; G. Lazian, *Heghapokhakan demker* [Revolutionary figures] (Cairo, 1949), pp. 285-293. A. Ter Minassian, "Le Mouvement revolutionnaire arménien," in *La Question Arménienne* (Rocqueaire, France, 1983), pp. 113-167.

[66] A. Ter Minassian, "Le Mouvement Revolutionnaire Arménien." Harsh verdicts were given in the trial of Kukunian in 1893. Arrests of Hunchaks occurred in 1895.

[67] *PSDHK*, p. 36.

[68] For the Kurds, see M. Varandian, *HHDP*, Vol. I, pp. 254-258; K. Sasuni, *Kurd azgayin sharzhumnere ev haykrtakan haraberutiunnere* [The Kurdish national movements and Armeno-Kurdish relations] (Beirut, 1969). As for the Turks, "negotiations" carried on with the Young Turks in Paris, Geneva, and London.

[69] The word *fedayee* has a slightly mystical ring to it which is reminiscent of the original meaning of the word "martyr."

[70] C.J. Walker, *art. cit.*, pp. 22 et passim.

[71] R. Luxemburg, *art. cit.*

[72] A. Beylerian, "L'impérialisme et le mouvement national arménien (1885-1890)," *Relations Internationales* (Paris), 3(1975):19-54.

[73] P.I. Lyaschenko, *History of the National Economy of Russia to 1917* (New York, 1970), pp. 619-634.

[74] *Ibid.*

[75] Ronald G. Suny, *The Baku Commune 1917-1918* (Princeton, 1972), p. 7.

[76] *Ibid.*, p. 14.

[77] P.I. Lyaschenko, *op. cit.*, p. 631.

[78] B. Ishkhanian, *Nationaler Bestand, berufmässige Gruppierung und soziale Gliederung der Kaukasischen Völker* (Berlin, 1914).

[79] *Ibid.*, pp. 12-13, 21.

[80] D. Anunun, *op. cit.*, p. 90.

[81] V.A. Barsamian, *op. cit.*, Vol. III, p. 394.

[82] M. Varandian, *Hosankner* (Currents) (Geneva, 1910), p. 156.

[83] M.K. Kevonian, *art. cit.*, pp. 194-224.

[84] A. Ter Minassian, "Aux origines . . .," p. 72.

[85] *Ibid.*, p. 73. In a similar situation, see the behavior of Lebanese workers today. *Etat et perspective de l'industrie au Liban* (Beirut, 1978), pp. 37 et passim.

[86] V.A. Parsamian, *op. cit.*, Vol. III, pp. 348 et seq.

[87] *Ibid.*

[88]K. Gharibdjanian, *V.I. Lenine ev Andrkovkase* [V.I. Lenin and Transcaucasia] (Erevan, 1970), Vol. I, pp. 136 et seq.

[89]Bogdan Gnuniantz (1878-1911), one of the founders of the Baku Committee, was delegate to the London congress (1903) and member of the executive committee of the St. Petersburg Soviet (1905).

[90]Stepan Shahumian (1878-1918). K. Mamikonian, *Hay Sotsial Demokratneri Miutiune 1902-1903* [The Union of Armenian SDs 1902-1903] (Erevan, 1969). Cited pp. 98 et passim.

[91]K. Gharibdjanian, *op. cit.*, Vol. I, pp. 160-163.

[92]Al.R. (A. Rubeni) in *Sotsialist* (Geneva), no. 18-19, 1906, p. 27.

[93]Cited by M. Varandian, *HHDP*, p. 324.

[94]Aknuni, *op. cit.*, pp. 277-286.

[95]*Ibid.*, pp. 287-321; Ananun, *op. cit.*, Vol. III, pp. 35-42.

[96]M. Varandian, *HHDP*, Vol. I, p. 336.

[97]M. Varandian, *HHDP*, Vol. I, pp. 368-369. See the execution of Governor Nakashidze in Baku.

[98]*PSDHK*, pp. 413-421. D. Ananun, "L'orientation des hentchakians vers la révolution et le socialisme," *Nork* (Erevan, 1924), pp. 274-315.

[99]52 issues between June 1903 and June 1904.

[100]A. Ter Minassian, "Aux origines . . ."

[101]D. Ananun, *op. cit.*, Vol. III, p. 93; G. Haupt, *op. cit.*, p. 162.

[102]A. Ter Minassian, "Aux origines . . .," p. 80.

[103]*Ibid.*, pp. 76-78.

[104]K. Gharibdjanian, *op. cit*, Vol. I, p. 223.

[105]*Ibid.*, Vol. I, pp. 236-238.

[106]Al. Rubeni, *Sotsialist* (Geneva), no. 18-19, 1906, p. 28.

[107]Al. Rubeni, "Les systemes d'organisation de la Social Démocratie," *Kiank* (Life) (Tiflis), nos. 13-16, 1906.

[108]*Kiank* and later *Tsayn* (Voice) were the Specifist organs in Tiflis during 1906-1907.

[109] *Draft program, system of organization, statutes of the ASDWO* (in Armenian), n.d., n.p.

[110] Kh. Barseghian, *Bolshevikian hay barberakan mamuli bibliografia 1900-1920* [Bibliography of the Armenian Bolshevik press 1900-1920] (Erevan, 1959).

[111] V.A. Parsamian, *op. cit.*, Vol. III, p. 400.

[112] During the period when he was made responsible by Lenin for Armenian-language SD publications in Geneva.

[113] The best of the Armenian SD periodicals.

[114] Stalin, *Oeuvres* (Paris, 1975), Vol. I, pp. 40-56.

[115] Ashot Hovhannisian, *Engelse ev haykakan hartse* [Engels and the Armenian Question] (Moscow, 1931).

[116] S. Shahumian, *op. cit.*, based his argument on K. Kautsky's article, "La question nationale en Russie" (1905).

[117] See *PSDHK*, Vol. I, on 4th, 5th congresses. *Hunchak* opened the debate in September 1903 (no. 13-14) with an article "On the New Action."

[118] Published in Paris from January to August 1905.

[119] R. Khan Azat, *art. cit.*

[120] It was a creation of Kristapor Mikayelian.

[121] This behavior was harshly judged by D. Ananun.

[122] Hrach Dasnabedian, ed., *Niuter HH patmutian hamar* [Sources for the History of the ARF] (Beirut, 1974), Vol. II, pp. 104-192.

[123] Organized by Kristapor Mikayelian (who was killed accidentally in Bulgaria during the 1905 preparations), the attempted assassination of the Sultan failed in July 1905.

[124] *Niuter . . .*, Vol. II, pp. 205-223.

[125] *Ibid.*, p. 210.

[126] *HHDP*, Vol. I, pp. 358-435; A. Gulghandian, *Hay tatarakan enthanrumnere* [The Armeno-Tatar Clashes] (Paris, 1933); D. Ananun, *op. cit.*, Vol. III, pp. 165-264; Aknuni, *op. cit.*, pp. 323-335; etc.

[127] A. Ter Minassian, "Aux origines . . .," p. 83.

[128] R.G. Hovannisian, *Armenia on the Road to Independence, 1918* (Berkeley, 1967), p. 21.

[129] Kh. Barseghian, op. cit., pp. 50-54.

[130] Naro, "Trois mois," Tsayn (Tiflis), nos. 4, 5, 6, 1906.

[131] Niuter . . ., Vol. II, pp. 232-236.

[132] Richard, "Why we are leaving the Dashnaktsutiun," Erkri Tsayne, (Tiflis), no. 14, 1907.

[133] Murj was a liberal and democratic monthly published in Tiflis from 1889 to 1907.

[134] From the name of a fedayee leader, Mihran, who was a native of Turkey.

[135] V. Minakhorian, "Anjatakannere" (The Separatists) Vem 2(1933).

[136] A. Amirian, Jamanakn e stapvelu (It is time to wake up) (Vienna, 1906); Dachnaksutian krizise (The crisis in the Dashnaktsutiun) (Vienna, 1907).

[137] Levon Atabekian had been one of the great hopes of the Dashnak party.

[138] Niuter . . ., Vol. III.

[139] R. Pipes, The formation of the Soviet Union (Cambridge, 1970), p. 28.

[140] Admitted initially as a Caucasian party and then from 1909 as the representative of Turkish Armenia.

[141] Mikayel Varandian (1874-1934). The most fruitful theoretician of the Dashnak party and its historian. Member of the Western Bureau and editor of Droshak.

[142] G. Haupt, op. cit., pp. 135-138.

[143] See the Armenian satirical press in Tiflis during 1906 through 1907. In particular, Khatabala.

[144] M. Varandian, Hosankner, p. 139 et passim.

[145] A number of SD or Dashnak reviews were entitled Nor Hosank (New Current or New Way).

[146] R. Suny, op. cit., p. 50.

[147] A. Ter Minassian, "Aux origines . . .," pp. 92-93.

[148] Kh. Barseghian, op. cit.

[149] G. Hovhannisian, op. cit., p. 22.

[150] Published in the preface to his *Hayots parberakan mamule, 1794-1934* [The Armenian periodical press, 1794-1934] (Erevan, 1934).

[151] A. Amurian, *H.H. Dashnaktsutiun Parskastanum 1890-1918* [The ARF in Persia 1890-1918] (Teheran, 1950).

[152] They worked on the review *Erkri Tsayne* (The Voice of the Country) published by Tigrane Zaven in Tiflis from 1906 to 1908; these themes were elaborated in it.

[153] Reported by *Erkri Tsayne* and by *Alik* (Wave), the organ of the Dashnak party in Tiflis (1906-1907).

[154] *Andjumans* means district or town councils.

[155] "Déclaration du congres des Partis d'opposition de l'Empire ottoman réuni en Europe" (Décembre 1907) (Paris, 1908).

[156] For these problems there is no substitute for reading the daily *Azatamart* (Fight for freedom) published in Constantinople by the Dashnak party from 1909 onward.

[157] In particular, for the role of Armenians in the Iranian social democratic movement see S. Ravasani, *Sowjetrepublik Gilan Die Sozialestisches Bewegieng im Iran seit Eude des 19. jhdt bis 1922* (Berlin, 1974); C. Chaqueri, *La Social-Démocratie en Iran* (Florence, 1979).

[158] M. Varandian, *HHDP*, Vol. II. In the Armenian press, Dashnak or non-Dashnak, countless articles were devoted to Eprem Khan (Eprem Davidiants, 1869-1912) between 1909 and 1912.

[159] D. Ananun, *op. cit.*, Vol. III, pp. 507-530; R.G. Hovannisian, "The Armenian Question in the Ottoman Empire," *Armenian Studies* (Beirut, 1973), pp. 1-25.

[160] The Armenian bourgeoisie dominated the Tiflis and Baku Dumas. In the fourth state Duma, the two Armenian deputies were Kadets.

[161] This "rallying" and support are particularly clear in *Pro Armenia*, which was published with the title *For the Peoples of the East* from December 1912 in a bilingual edition (French-English). In issue no. 3 (1912), Victor Berard justified the new Russian policy in an article entitled "Le choix arménien:" "We are being massacred in Turkey,

Russia is satisfied with oppressing us; it is still better to live under Russian law than to perish in an Ottoman massacre."